Cycle Touring For Beginners

A GUIDE TO EXPLORING NEAR AND FAR
BY BICYCLE

Marie Madigan

Wood Sorrel Books

Book Layout ©2013 BookDesignTemplates.com

Thank you for supporting the work of this author.
Please consider leaving a review wherever you bought the book, or telling your friends about it, to help spread the word.
Sign up for the author's New Releases mailing list and get a free digital copy of *A Short Ride Round North Wales*. Visit the website for more: www.mariemadigan.co.uk

Cycle Touring For Beginners / Marie Madigan. —1st ed.
ISBN 9781512114188

Contents

For Adi

You can't buy happiness but you can buy a bicycle, and that's pretty close.

—ANON

Introduction

I passionately believe that adventures are under our noses, wherever we live. I equally passionately believe that riding a bike is one of the loveliest ways of getting around. My home is in Wales now and if I wanted I could ride for a lifetime just in Britain and Ireland and still find new places to explore. I can't believe my luck that I was born here, that I continue to live here, and that I have all this country under my nose.

This applies wherever you live: fifteen miles down the road, if you go there by bicycle and stay overnight, will give a sense of newness and discovery. I think it's a great shame that someone might not try cycle touring because they think that:

a. you can't do it unless you're really fit and have a year off, and

b. you can't have an adventure just by going out of your front door and riding down the road to familiar places.

I wrote this book because there are many fine books and websites on cycle touring out there. But most of them talk about 'tour' as in 'expedition'. Across Europe. Trans-Saharan. Alaska to Tierra del Fuego.

My aim is to show you that cycle touring is a wonderful way to see the world, both nearby and faraway. To show you that you don't have to plan a monster tour to enjoy touring by bicycle. One night, one week, one month, one year: they are all cycle tours. The scale is up to you. I wrote this book to encourage you to try it for yourself as soon as possible, and to help you to avoid making some of the mistakes I've made.

With a bike, a few pieces of equipment and a spirit of curiosity, you can have an adventure riding from your place of work to your home. You can ride to a bed-and-breakfast or campsite in your local area, taking in that tea-shop that you've driven past for years. You can spend the night in a town or village you know only slightly, explore it, and ride home the next day by roads you'd normally never travel along in your car. You can discover what's under your nose, or what's on the other side of the country. If the inclination strikes you and you like starting big, of course you can start with a three-month ride around Europe, or across North America. Cycle touring is wonderful, the most magical way of seeing the world around you, and anyone can do it. It doesn't have to be a ten-week ride. That's just a ride. They're all just rides. You can start one.

Looking down at your legs and then back at where you've just come from and thinking, 'We did that. You and me, Legs,' is one of the most ridiculously simple and satisfying things in life.

Anyone can do it. Anyone.

All you need is a bicycle.

CHAPTER 1

Is This Book For You?

This book is aimed mainly at people who may be thinking about cycle touring for the first time, but it will also be of use if you've already been on a few trips and are planning a more adventurous tour. It will focus on things to consider when planning a trip of any length, from the point of view of someone who's gradually learnt how not to make life harder for herself over seven years of touring.

There are many companies now who will organise a cycle tour for you, from planning the route to carrying your luggage on for you at night. Some of them will set up food stations for you during the day, so you only need to carry a little food on the bike. These are particularly popular in the stunningly lovely Pyrenean and Alpine mountains that feature in the Tour de France every year. Often these companies describe themselves as *cyclo*-touring companies rather than **cycle touring**; that little e-to-o substitution makes it clear that it is the sporting aspect that is emphasised, rather than the touring aspect.

In contrast to cyclo-tourers, cycle tourers are almost always independent, valuing the freedom to change their minds, to ride faster or slower as landscape or weather or mood dictates. They carry their own baggage, make up their own routes and sort out their own food.

In case you are getting nervous, let me reassure you that you don't have to be on a shoe-string budget to enjoy an independent cycle tour. You can eat and stay in the best accommodation your chosen destination or route has to offer if that's what you fancy. Credit card or tiny tent – both are independent and highly rewarding. Cycle touring isn't about punishing yourself, it's about seeing the world, whether near or far, from the back of your bike. If the thought of doing without your luxuries is already putting you off, take them with you! I certainly don't do without mine. Book into those luxury hotels if you want to.

Over the years I've met cycle tourers in many forms, all riding with their own quests, whether that's a weekend ride around the coast of an island or a multi-week trip. I've had my hastily formed pre-conceptions overturned by enormous plump men riding slowly but unstoppably up Pyrenean inclines; by slim and flinty-eyed lycra-clad young men who turned out to be unexpectedly rhapsodic about the beauties of the countryside; by relaxed-looking baggy-trousered sorts who've pinned me into a corner to recite their trip log-book at me. ('Two hundred kilometres in two days – how many k's do you do in a day?')

Couples from their twenties to their seventies. Families. Lone women linking the landmarks of Spain in a steady plod. Groups of friends following the route of the Tour de France.

If they can do it, you can.

If I can do it, you can.

For seven years I've made all the mistakes – eaten the wrong food on the bike, or not enough, carried too much, carried too little – actually no, that's a lie, I've never carried too little. But I've forgotten to stretch, failed to prepare properly, neglected to bring gloves to Scottish islands, left maps at home, and I've survived. And in the process I've gradually learned how to make things a little easier for myself.

An hour and a half into my first cycle tour I wobbled into a hedge half way up a hill and wondered what the hell I was doing. Four days later I'd crossed northern England from coast to coast, on a bike I now know was set up for someone half my height with thighs twice as long as mine. I hadn't been wearing padded shorts so I was, well, a bit sore. But I was ecstatic. I'd crossed the country, sea to sea, just me, my bike and my legs.

Since then my partner Adi and I have ridden extensively in northern England, Scotland's highlands and islands, Wales, Ireland and France, with forays into Italy and Spain. We've ridden across Anglesey for a night on the west coast and ridden back the next day; we've twice cycled through France for two months. I can't imagine going on holiday without a bike now. I can scarcely imagine a holiday that isn't a cycle tour.

I want to persuade you to try cycle touring, to experience that same thrill of discovering the world around you by bicycle that I've discovered over the last seven years, armed with advice to help you to avoid making the mistakes I've made.

Green, active, as slow or as fast as you like, endowing independence and autonomy, the bicycle is one of the pinnacles of human achievement. Add panniers and it's a vehicle of exploration as well!

Just in case you're still not convinced, here are some reasons to try cycle touring.

1. You can lock your bike, hide it behind a hedge and take a break from it to go for a walk. When you're cycle touring, you can explore on foot as well. Two modes for the price of one.

2. You can ride as quickly as you need to make that ferry/train/plane, to eat up miles if you're relishing the physicality, or choose to ride slowly enough to really take in your surroundings:

lizards scuttling at the side of the road, interesting ruins in a field. You can feel the shape of the country changing underneath you.

3. You'll get stronger as you do it, in spite of yourself. Unless you're dreadfully unlucky, it is impossible to end a cycle tour less fit than you were when you started.

4. You can eat puddings with impunity. I am a huge fan of tea shops and cakes, but I like to earn those treats. Cycle touring is no-questions-asked credit in the cake equations.

5. You'll experience the kindness of strangers. There's something about turning up somewhere on a travel-stained, pannier-laden bike that stimulates people's curiosity and sense of hospitality; before you know it, you are deep in conversation with total strangers. By the same token, it's easier to ask for help when you need it; people seem predisposed to help you when you are in the sometimes vulnerable position of carrying your worldly goods with you on your bike.

6. It turns down the chatter in your mind. Most of us live with a constant, never-ending list of things that we must do – job, cooking, cleaning, civilising children and pets. Cycle touring pares life down to the essentials – reaching shelter and finding food – giving you time to admire your surroundings, enjoy the fresh air and exercise or just to zone out into an almost meditative state where nothing matters but the turning of the pedals.

When it comes down to it, here's all you really need to start cycle touring:

1. A working bicycle
2. Waterproof luggage
3. Curiosity
4. Will

These alone will get you out the door and on your way. The type of bicycle really doesn't matter as long as you can reach the pedals and the brakes work. A rucksack, while not ideal, will do for luggage if you have nothing else. And curiosity and will: well, all you need to do is roll out of your house, knowing that you are now under your own steam and in control of your own destiny.

A tourer I met once told me the story that inspired him to try it. At a campsite in Devon one evening he bumped into a man in his fifties who'd saved up his year's allowance of holidays, borrowed his son's bike and a mate's sleeping bag and bivouac sack, strapped a sports bag to the rear rack and set off. He was trying to see how far around Devon and Cornwall he could get in three weeks. Not everyone's cup of tea, but swap the bivvy sack for a tent or a credit card and it illustrates the main point of this book:

Get a bike. Pick somewhere to go to. Saddle up and start pedalling.

If you are even now looking out the window, itching to grab a map of your area and see how far you could get tonight – excellent! I am delighted. Put this aside, don't let the feeling fade. Enjoy your ride. Come back to this another time. Tell me how you get on – I'd love to know.

If, on the other hand, you'd like to know more about ways to make the experience as easy and painless as possible, read on.

CHAPTER 2

The Bike

There are plenty of excellent specialised touring bikes available but unless you are dying to spend a couple of thousand pounds right now, chances are you own or can borrow a perfectly adequate bicycle.

Not to labour the point (but I will), all you really need is a bike that rolls forward when you push on the pedals, bags to keep your stuff in, and the willingness to do it. Make sure the seat isn't too high or too low, or that the frame isn't too big for you and that the brakes work, and you're good to go. Once you've tried cycle touring and fallen in love with it, taking the time to find some good, reliable components will make things easier for you, but always remember: if you get carried away you'll be spending precious riding time inside poring over images of shiny wonder-kit that probably won't help that much unless you're planning some sort of personal best assault on the Land's End to John O'Groats. At some point you've got to say, 'This'll do', get on the bike and go. Sometimes good enough really is good enough.

This chapter covers the main kinds of bicycle available, as well as a note on bike fit and gearing, notes on components such as tyres and handlebars, and a brief word about bicycle maintenance.

Types of bike

1. Touring bikes
2. Hybrid/commuting bikes
3. Mountain bikes
4. Road bikes
5. Unusual-shaped bikes. This includes tandems.

1. Touring bikes

Specialised touring bikes have sturdy frames and wheels, with plenty of lugs designed to take pannier racks front and rear. A relaxed frame geometry with a long wheel-base is designed to maximise comfort for long periods in the saddle. They may or may not have drop handlebars.

Traditional expedition touring bikes were made of steel, and many still are, for the simple reason that it can be welded. This a boon if you are travelling in remote areas in Asia, Africa and South America, for example, where your travel alternatives may be limited, where you are utterly dependent on your bike, and where getting a helpful welder to weld the broken bits back together might be your only way out of your predicament. However, if you're travelling in the UK, Europe, even the more isolated areas of countryside, you'll probably be within a few miles of a house or farm, somewhere you can knock on a door and ask for help, or where you can ring a taxi or emergency services from your mobile if you have to. Steel is not a great advantage in these circumstances.

2. Hybrid/commuting bikes

Hybrid bikes combine features of both road bikes and mountain bikes. Most commuting bikes fall into the hybrid category. Features derived from mountains bikes include a more upright riding position, flat handlebars and a stouter frame designed to take a wider tyre than a standard road bike. The gearing is more like road bikes, with a wide range for faster riding on flats while being able to go up hills easily (easily being a relative term). Hybrids also inherited lighter components, wheel rims and spokes from road bikes.

I still use my 13-year-old Dawes Tanami, essentially a commuting bike. My partner Adi always tours on his beloved Marin Sausalito hybrid, which has front suspension. He almost always rides with the suspension fully locked down.

Commuting bikes and touring bikes have a lot in common, the frame geometry and construction being designed to cope with frequent encounters with kerbs and potholes. Subtle differences in the angles formed by the tubes of the frame make touring bikes more comfortable to ride for prolonged periods, but really, this is the sort of thing that, if you've never had it, you won't miss it.

Most hybrids come with lugs (little holes on the frame) for attaching a rear rack, if they don't come already supplied with one.

3. Road bikes

If you like the idea of riding light, are planning to stay in comfortable accommodation like hostels and B&Bs and always eat out, then all you'll need to carry will be your clothes. Some road bikes have lugs so that a small, neat rack can be affixed – you can get racks specifically designed for the slender-waisted road bike now – which means that panniers can be carried. Bear in mind that you really need to keep the weight down if you choose to do this, as the light wheel rims, hubs and spokes are not designed to bear weight. We once met a young Irish couple riding the Pyrenees west to east. The woman was carrying nothing but water bottles; the man was pulling a trailer. (I was fascinated. Where had they put all their books?) For them, the whole reason for the tour was getting up and down as many mountain passes as possible, for which their road bikes and trailer were perfect. Another young man we met on a road bike was travelling with nothing more than a teeny rucksack on his back, to which he'd strapped a bivvy bag and a baguette. He wore the most beatific expression as he told us of the region in the Alps north of Liguria that he was heading for. He was the only person I've met who combined sheer Grand Tour-level fitness with an obvious love for the landscape, in contrast to the steely-eyed, grit-toothed col- and kilometre-counters that abound in France's hilly regions.

But I digress. If you're contemplating touring on a road bike you probably haven't read this far anyway and are off planning your ten thousand metres of ascent in two days. Good luck to you. But rest assured you can, with credit-card travelling, get away with a couple of very light panniers.

4. Mountain bikes

Mountain bikes open up a whole world of off-road touring. In the UK, the extensive network of public bridleways added to the road network increases the choice of routes and adventures enormously. The most exciting bridleways are tougher than the sturdiest of hybrids can cope with, and can only be enjoyed on a proper mountain bike. Luggage racks that will fit over both front and rear suspension are easily available now, and if you're travelling light, or just trying it out for the first time, a medium-sized rucksack might be enough. One caveat though: a road tour on a mountain bike will be much more energy-sapping than on a road bike, with all your energy disappearing into the suspension rather than sending you forwards. If you've got a mountain bike, use it for a mostly off-road tour, where it will shine.

5. Unusual-shaped bikes: recliners, tricycles, tandems and the like

I'm including tandems here because I think there's nothing weirder than taking all the magic of the bicycle, all its potential for independence and autonomy and emancipation, and using that magic to shackle yourself to another autonomous, independent and emancipated person with opinions of their own, such as on when to stop, for example, when they are in front with access to the brakes and you are not. But many enjoy them, and you can get an awful lot of panniers on a tandem. We have met people travelling on recliners, recliner-upright tandem combinations, tricycles and on one memorable occasion, a reclining tricycle with a sail. This young man was racing up through France, doing 200 km a day and attracting some attention from police helicopters clearly trying to work out whether or not he was legal. He'd had no direct approaches so presumably he was okay!

The point is, you can try cycle touring on any kind of bike you have lying around or can borrow. Remember, it's not about the bike. It's about having a go.

Gearing

Almost anywhere you cycle will bring you face to face with gradients: big hills, little hills, long energy-sapping hills, unexpected tiny vicious slopes hiding around corners. No matter how disciplined you are with your packing, these will be tougher with panniers, and you'll find yourself using the lower range of gears a lot more often.

Make it easier on yourself from the beginning, if you can. Once you know you enjoy cycle touring (and you will, you will! Just try it!), invest in a chainset designed to cope with hills. You might have heard cyclists speak about the granny ring; this is the lowest gear on your bike, and it's worth making sure it is the grandmother of all granny rings. My Dawes now has a triple chainset on the front with 46-34-24 teeth, rather than the fairly standard 48-38-28 that it came with. Together with my rear cassette – nine rings ranging from 11 teeth to 34 – this means that I should be able to ride up a telegraph pole. Before acquiring this configuration about four years ago I often had cause, plodding along in bottom gear in hilly regions, to look down between my struggling knees in the hope that another, lower gear had miraculously grown. With my current arrangement I've only experienced that horrible sensation twice. I've been up 25% hills on it – painfully slowly, with pauses to replace my popping eyeballs, but still going forwards. I can't recommend a good set of low gears enough, especially if you're small. Even though I'm fit now, everyone I go riding with has at least 50% more muscle in their thighs than I do. I love my granny ring; I urge you to find a granny ring you love as well.

Don't listen to the assistants in the bike shop. It's my experience that, with a few honourable exceptions, bike shop staff don't tend to be tourers and have little experience of carrying a tent, clothes, cooking stove, food and sleeping stuff in hilly regions. If they tell you they go cycle touring, you can bet your house on it they mean cyclo-touring. And you and I know the world of difference that little 'o' makes.

Bike fitting

Bike fitting means making sure that the adjustable components – saddle height and position, handlebar height, length of pedal crank – are adjusted for your body shape. Good fit will prevent injury and strain, and will make your riding more efficient. (If the word 'efficient' is turning you off, don't worry. I won't use it too often. But bear in mind that the easier your riding is on your body, the more distance you can get for your effort, which means in turn more time at your disposal to dawdle when you choose to, to enjoy that afternoon tea and cake or pint, instead of constantly chasing the night and the light to get to your resting place.)

Saddle height

The golden rule is that it's better to have your saddle set too low than too high; an overly high saddle really will cause your muscles some grief, if not actual strain and damage. For my part, it wasn't until summer 2013 that I finally abandoned the sit-up-and-beg posture that I'd adopted all my life. Photos show me grinning up hills (always smile into the camera when riding up a hill), my bum very obviously lower than my hands. I didn't know anything else, I liked it that way, and I'd cycled all around Scotland and its islands, from the south to the north of France, and up some fearsome hills with my seat a good three inches lower than my handlebars. Over the past couple of years I've become accustomed to a lower riding position, mostly as a result of acquiring and loving a slim little road bike, and I've raised the saddle and lowered the handlebars of my Dawes; this makes things a bit easier on my body when swapping from bike to bike. No doubt I'd have been a bit better off in terms of efficiency if I'd adopted this riding position for cycle touring a few years ago, but the point is, I survived without undue aches and pains. And I enjoyed thousands of miles of travelling.

Saddle position

Saddle position front-to-back is the one that will really make a difference. Take the time to slide your seat forwards and backwards on the rails, a couple of millimetres at a time. Yes, really, a couple of millimetres. Your lower back can tell the difference.

Crank length

It wasn't until four years ago, when I replaced my original front chainset for the lower-geared set mentioned above, that I realised that I'd been riding for years with pedal cranks designed for someone with thighs a foot longer than mine. Up until then I'd just replaced it like for like. 'How tall are you?' asked the man from Spa Cycles when I rang up to order a replacement. 'What?' He sent one 15 mm shorter. Having a less-than-perfect pedal crank length isn't going to spoil your first cycle tour, but it's the sort of thing you could consider when you come to replace your chainrings. A different length of crank might suit your shape more.

It's worth remembering that your body is very good at letting you know when something isn't fitting correctly. Listen to your body; learn to distinguish the comfortable ache of a well-exercised muscle from the niggling pain of a strained one, and make some adjustments to your seat and handlebars position.

If you want to look further into bike fitting, there are a number of companies that will do a professional bike fit for you; a quick Google search will bring up at least one in your area. Less expensively, typing 'bike fit' into YouTube will bring up plenty of instructional videos on the subject. Cycling magazines often have advice on how to set your bike up yourself, in a bit more detail than the 'knee slightly bent' trick of received wisdom.

But remember the golden rule: good enough is good enough. Don't wait for perfection. Those roads are waiting.

Helpful components

Pedals

For the last three years I have been using two-sided touring pedals, which are flat on one side and cleated on the other. This means I can use them with my cleated sandals or shoes, or flip them over if I'm wearing ordinary footwear. It's important to point out that these are touring, or leisure, dual pedals, where both the cleated side and the flat side have a large surface area. Some dual pedals are much smaller, meant for road bikes.

I find that the cleats tend to help on long, steady rides on the flat or on very gentle uphill slopes, as you can pull upwards with your hamstrings as well as push down with your quadriceps. However, it's not something to get hung up about.

Handlebars

Many touring bikes have drop handlebars, offering alternative hand and body positions. Others, and most hybrids, come fitted with flat handlebars. Often they have extensions, the so-called cow horns that fit onto the ends of the handlebar and protrude forward, again offering variations on your hand position. On long rides this can be invaluable, as it gives your hands, arms, shoulders and upper back the chance to change position, to wriggle around and avoid getting stiff. Using the cow horns also helps to open out your rib cage, making breathing easier on hard hills, for example. Taking this even further, you can acquire touring handlebars, also known as 'butterfly' bars. Adi invested in these some years ago and swears by them; as there is twice as much handlebar as normal, there are twice as many places to rest your hands, as well as to fix accessories such as bar bag, bike computer and lamps.

If you're going to be cycling in a hot climate don't, I implore you, use foam handlebar grips. There is no feeling more stomach-turning than, freshly fed and washed of a morning, placing clean hands upon handlebars saturated with a mixture of sunscreen, sweat and rain. Utterly, utterly gross.

Tyres

Punctures are a nuisance. Once we'd started touring and knew that we were never going to stop we researched various forums on the internet and went with the most consistently recommended brand. We've been using Schwalbe Marathons ever since, and have seen no reason to change. They seem to be puncture-repellent, combining sturdiness and a decent tread with efficiency for long rides.

A word about bicycle maintenance

If you have any fears about your ability to keep a bike in working order, it might cheer you to know that my partner Adi is rolling around on the ground laughing at the thought that I am about to give rudimentary bike maintenance advice.

Bike maintenance for years fell into the 'I-know-I-should-but' category of things to do. To say I did the minimum is a laughable understatement, and if there was any justice in the universe I'd be ending this paragraph with the sentence, 'But I've learned the hard way that...' I did not learn the hard way. My bike loyally carried me for years with minimal attention. However, once I started touring and riding a lot more, I started to consult YouTube from where I learnt to replace worn out chainrings and the like myself. I still fall short of my own precepts, but I'm riding a bike that I've owned for thirteen years, and it still does everything I ask of it.

Significant maintenance issues are way beyond the scope of this book. However, the more care you've taken of your bike before you head off on your trip, the less chance there is of something failing halfway through or – even more infuriatingly – half a mile after setting out. I highly recommend the wonderful *Total Bike Maintenance Book* by Mel Allwood. Clear pictures, for-numpties language, simplified as far as possible but no further, this is now my bible. Under its guidance I have managed to service headsets (a hidden part of whose existence I had only the haziest grasp a couple of years ago), remove and refit chainrings and cassettes, even index my rear derailleur. But remember: **you don't have to know all this in order to start.** I didn't know what a bottom bracket was until Adi's started creaking on a tour of the Western Isles six years ago. I had only the haziest grasp of how the handlebars connect to the fork until, under Mel's kindly guidance, I dismantled everything at the front end.

All that being said, we have evolved a short check that we go through every few days when we're out on a long tour.

Longer tour maintenance check list

1. Check brake pads for wear. Remove accumulated gunk and give the rims a quick scrub.

2. Check tyres for bits of glass, sharp grit or thorns; sometimes these take a while to work through to the inner tube, so punctures can be avoided by catching them early.

3. Wipe chain clean of dirt. Strictly, this should be every day in order to avoid build-up of dirt sticking to the oil, but I never manage a daily check. Oil chain if necessary.

4. Check all the little bolts holding pannier racks on and tighten if necessary.

5. Clean off as much crud as possible.

6. Wipe handlebars clean, for the reasons mentioned above. This is the one thing that I do without fail.

As long as you know how to repair a puncture and replace your brake pads, and you are carrying a mobile phone, a £20 note and some small change in case you have to use a pay phone, there's nothing stopping you. You don't need to have a touring bike or know how to fix it. You can try cycle touring this weekend.

The short way to the best bike to start cycle touring

Remember this: despite the massively long crank arms and too-low seat position, I'd had three thoroughly enjoyable years of cycle touring on my not-designed-for-touring bike before I played around with the components. You can too.

Dust off your bike. Oil the chain. Check your brakes. Pump the tyres up. Go for a ride, then a longer one. Go for the night twenty miles down the road. All you need is a bike.

CHAPTER 3

Fitness And Health

This section addresses two questions often asked by non-cycle tourers.

a. How fit should you be to start cycle touring?
b. How do you stay healthy on the road?

How fit should you be when you start?

If you have serious concerns about your health, or have any kind of condition that impacts upon your life daily, then you should seek your doctor's advice before doing this, as you would before undertaking any strenuous new activity.

I maintain that cycle touring is wonderful for those of an idle disposition, because of the many opportunities for idling that it presents. It follows that you don't need to be freakishly fit to enjoy it.

In the Pyrenees in 2013, our route for three or four days coincided with that of Bruce the Canadian. Bruce was not a small man.

Bruce was not a thin man. But Bruce was on a month-long tour of his own, including the route of Stage 9 of that year's Tour de France, which we were also following, and which went over five major passes. Bruce was going to do them all, and do them he did. I have never seen anyone move more slowly on a bike and still keep it up-right. He never stopped. He was incredible.

He had will.

That's all you need.

If you don't believe that, maybe putting it this way sounds more convincing: cycle touring makes you fitter against your will. You can do things to help, but you do not need to be super-fit when you start out. Repeated exercise, even if you are not pushing yourself, does burn more calories and make you fitter. It's not just the cycling: sim-ply being outside, hopping on and off and wheeling the bike through crowded town centres on wet August days when everyone's looking for something dry to do, for example, uses up lots of energy. And if you are camping there's all the extra exercise that doesn't feel like exercise: pitching your tent, sorting out your bedding, rooting out your clean clothes and wash things, showering, preparing and cook-ing your dinner – these all take time and effort, and nibble away at your excess poundage. And there's all that lifting of panniers onto the bike in the morning before you set off. Great for the biceps.

But please remember: getting fitter is a pleasant bonus. It need not be the main reason (though it's not a bad one) and I believe you'd be losing out on some of the loveliest and most pleasurable aspects of cycle touring if it was. I believe that cycle touring is wonderful be-cause you will see the world in a way you had not seen it before.

The best way to work out how fit you are for the sort of touring you want to do is to choose somewhere you would like to go, and cycle there. Ride slowly, take breaks, go at a comfortable pace. You'll get used to the feel of the bike with panniers on and you'll work out what pace suits you best. You'll discover whether you're happier pushing your bike up a long, attritional slope, whether you prefer to chug on stubbornly, or whether stopping for rests and starting again is better. The latter is actually the approach that will get you fitter faster, thus gradually making the whole experience more enjoyable. As the old-timer road cyclists say, 'don't buy upgrades, ride up grades': that is, up gradients. Which proves the point that it really isn't about the bike, and you can get fitter by cycle touring whatever sort of bike you ride. Stop to get your breath back, then get back on the bike and continue slowly until you have to stop again, even if you can only manage to ride for half a minute. As I don't have the strength to push my laden bike up a hill – panniers get in the way and I'm more afraid of straining my back than of straining my thighs – I have had no choice but to adopt this approach, and gradually it's made me much better at hills. A good streak of stubbornness helps as well.

But remember: you don't have to be super-fit when you start.

Staying healthy on the road

There are other considerations besides fitness. Just because you can do something really hard like ride seventy hilly miles into a head-wind doesn't mean that your body is going to thank you for it next morning, or next year, or in five years' time. Here are a few pointers to health and happiness on the road.

1. Hydration

This is covered in more detail in the section on food, but in short you should drink plenty of water. If you feel thirsty, you're already dehydrated. Long-term mild dehydration can be tough on your kidneys; try to stay ahead by taking regular sips from your water bottle. Staying hydrated means your body will process your food more effectively as well.

2. Stretching

This is another case of do-as-I-say-not-as-I-do, or, more kindly, something to which I am still aspiring. Adi and I have become much better over the last few years at stretching before and after cycling, but I think I speak for both of us when I say that we probably leave out either a morning or evening stretch on nearly half of our touring days, and some days we don't stretch at all. We overlooked stretching entirely for the first couple of years; we're so slow at getting going in the morning that by the time everything is packed away and the bikes are loaded, we're bouncing up and down, impatient to get rolling. (Or more truthfully, I'm the one bouncing up and down. Adi is much more patient.) Still, we have got better at doing a few moving stretches in the morning. It becomes easier to remember to do these when you ride out of your campsite and immediately slam your nose up against the vertical road that is your first challenge of the day, as is almost inevitable on Corsica, for example. If you are riding in easy terrain, gentle pedalling in an easy gear for the first ten or fifteen minutes will be enough to warm up your muscles. Never do static stretches before your muscles have warmed up. A quick Google search will pull up some results for dynamic, pre-cycling stretches. Be careful to watch them before you try them, and be sensible about matching them to your current level of athleticism. If you have any concerns discuss them with your doctor, or ask for advice at your local leisure centre.

Whilst touring, it's the post-ride stretch, generally agreed by sports scientists to be the more important one, that is more likely to be skipped. When you ride up to a campsite in the dark, late, hungry and tired, and the fact that your riding companion is the only person in the country that you know is all that's keeping you from making snippy remarks such as 'If we'd taken that turn three hours ago as I suggested...', your first thought is unlikely to be, 'Right, what I need is a good gluteus maximus stretch. Where's the yoga mat?'

My routine when getting to a campsite even slightly late runs something like this:

- Find toilet.
- Stuff half a baguette into mouth while unloading panniers.
- Get tent up.
- Sort out bedding while Adi has a shower.
- Have shower while Adi cooks.
- Eat dinner, trying not to gobble it.
- Start to feel like a human being once more.
- Exclaim, 'Oh, I forgot to stretch again.'

If you can remember to stretch, your muscles will thank you the next day. And it feels great, lying down on the ground after a long day, to let gravity take over on some static stretches.

There is plenty of excellent advice on post-ride stretching on websites and in magazines. Here are a few of my regulars. You may have some favourites you can adapt. As ever, seek medical advice if you have any concerns.

Back: I am certainly no expert, but the yoga cat-cow stretch really releases my back. The cobra position – lying on your front and raising your head, neck and chest off the ground – is also a good counter to the riding position, which can be tough on your upper back and neck.

Hamstrings: sit down with your legs stretched straight out in front and lower your head as close as possible to your knees. If you're flexible, this will be a doddle. I have never touched my toes in my life, but get the same benefit to my hamstrings by resting my head on my bent knees and then straightening my legs in tiny increments, breathing slowly. If I can persuade myself to do this for five minutes I find it immensely calming, and am much more inclined to chop vegetables (my usual contribution to the evening camping meals) once this is over.

Gluteal muscles, affectionately known as glutes. These form a complex of muscles that basically make up your buttocks, the biggest being the gluteus maximus. These muscles work very hard while cycling, are frequently ignored, and often at the root of aches in the bum. My favourite way to stretch these is to lie on my back, with both legs in the air and the ankle of one crossed over the knee of the other. Pulling the straight leg towards the chest deepens the stretch in the glutes in the crossed leg.

Quadriceps, affectionately known as quads: the powerhouse thigh muscles you see pistoning away under your nose. There are numerous stretches: one I like is lying flat on my back with the heel of the leg being stretched tucked right back under the buttock; gravity does most of the work here. If you have issues with your knees or find this too uncomfortable, standing on one leg and holding your foot behind you, as near to your buttock as you can, will work as well.

3. Skin care

If this sounds vain, it isn't! Out there in the sun and rain and wind, your skin will turn to leather if you don't look after it. Sweat, sunscreen and rain form a slick of goo perfect for trapping such unlovely airborne stuffs as road grit and unwary insects. The bicycle breeze might fool you into thinking you're not burning, so you do need to be aware of the need to re-apply sunscreen. As well as waterproof sunscreen of at least Factor 30, I bring an after-sun cream and body moisturiser, as well as face and hand moisturisers. I don't mind carrying enormous quantities of these.

I have listed the contents of my hair-and-skin care bag below. Apart from the sunscreen and body moisturisers, I decant most items into small containers and tubes (25-50 millilitres).

- Face moisturiser, suitable for day and night application
- Toothpaste and toothbrush
- Face wash
- Shower-gel
- Shampoo and conditioner
- After-sun and/or body moisturiser
- Miniature hairbrush that opens out with a tiny mirror
- Lip balm
- Deodorant

4. First Aid kit

You'll need at least a rudimentary medical kit for coping with minor mishaps. We carry a small one which, depending upon where we are, might contain:

- Painkillers such as paracetomol and ibuprofen. They don't interact with each other so that if you do get a headache or pains that need suppressing in order for you to battle on to where you need to be, you can take them at two-hourly intervals up to the maximum recommended each day.
- Assorted adhesive plasters, for small cuts and scrapes.
- Rectangular and triangular bandages, for larger wounds that might need to be kept covered for a few days. These non-adhesive bandages, secured with gauze, are much easier and

more pleasant to remove at the end of the day than sticking plasters.

- Sterile gauze, for binding bandages.
- Hydrocortisone/antihistamine creams, for the treatment of insect bites and stings.
- Small pair of scissors, for cutting bandages and gauze.
- Strong sunscreen, which must be waterproof.
- Insect repellent. When cycling in Scotland our favourite midge repellent is Avon Skin-So-Soft, a moisturising spray which all the forestry workers in Scotland have been using for years, mystifying Avon's sales department. For mosquitos and other biting insects of the Mediterranean regions, there is a great range of over-the-counter repellents. I can't stand the stuff, the chemicals being horrible, but so is being bitten, itching like mad in spite of having slathered yourself in equally horrible but supposedly soothing lotion to counter the effects of the bite, and then scratching the bites in your sleep anyway so that they ooze onto your sleeping bag liner. Dissuade the little beasts anyway you can, is my advice.
- Tweezers. Handy for extracting bits of road from your flesh after tumbles. Hopefully will remain unused for the duration of your trip. I've only actually parted company with my bike in mid-air twice in thousands of miles, and one of those resulted in gravel embedding itself in the sole of my foot. I removed the last clear sliver of quartz with my tweezers two days after the incident.

Warning: cycle touring can have some rather gross physical consequences.

Some of these can be revolting. I feel it's only fair to warn you.

July 2013. I'm riding along a Spanish road, lorries doing their best to give me space but still throwing up fountains of filthy spray. The morning started hot and sunny and I was soaked in sweat before ten o'clock as we crested a mountain pass, but as we descended the heavens opened. Now the tarmac is slick after the thunderstorm. The sky is lightening through the faint drizzle. It's still warm despite the rain, and I'm sweating lightly under my rain jacket as I try to keep up with Adi. We're approaching the outskirts of Bilbao, we have no map and we're getting very hungry. We follow signs for the city centre, stop at a bus stop and examine the map posted nearby and compare it with Google maps, which is taking forever to load and costing a fortune in roaming data charges. I'm too tired to think and have to trust in Adi's sense of direction as he takes off again through strange streets. At last the road curves down, there's a bridge and just across it looms the Guggenheim Museum and Gallery, its beaten metalwork surface gleaming as the sun comes fully out at last. Tourists wander in the plaza outside, going to the Tourist Information Office, stopping to take pictures of the enormous, endearing figure of a terrier formed entirely from hanging baskets. I sit on a bench and open my jacket. A fug almost physical enough to have a personality rolls out from my body. I look around, at the gardens sloping away from us, at the clean and well-dressed people, at the shining Museum where, I know, there are galleries free to enter, full of glorious works of art, and I think, 'I can't go in there. I absolutely ming.'

Cycling makes you dirty. If it's not sweat, it's rain, and if you discover that you are some sort of rain deity, as I'm convinced I am, it is often both. That day outside the Guggenheim it took ten minutes with a pack of fragrant wipes to clean my exposed bits of skin before I felt respectable enough to sneak into the Museum's café to use the toilet. Unstrapping my sandals revealed a distressing contrast between dark and light skin, less of a tan-line than a tide-line. My brown legs were slick with a mixture of sunscreen, sweat and rain, flecked all over with road-grit and fragments of unfortunate insects. This horrible coating was getting worse, if possible, as the weather improved, drying slowly into a thin crud over all my skin.

I was FILTHY.

This was not unusual.

If you go cycle touring, you will get dirty. You will pull up sometimes at lovely bars, pedalsore and thirsty, and you will be gasping for a drink, but you will be deterred from doing so by the knowledge that you and your aroma will clear the bar if you go inside.

The flipside of this is that you will enjoy getting clean as you have never enjoyed it before. Cycle touring offers many, many pleasures, and not the least of these is standing in a shower with far too much goopy shower gel and feeling the grime release its hold and slide away. You will feel reborn, a shiny personification of cleanliness born from the husk of an exhausted, hungry, filthy creature. On my various tours, the environmental kudos of months upon months of sustainable, green travel has probably been entirely negated by the volume of water I have consumed in showers, but it's been worth it.

If you've read this far, you probably won't get put off by the above.

Dust off your bike. Oil the chain. Bounce up and down on your toes, stretch your calves. Put a bag on the rack or on your back. Add a bottle of sunscreen for good luck. Stuff in a pack of sweet-smelling wipes. Choose a destination. Pedal away.

CHAPTER 4

Care and Feeding of the Cycle Tourer

This chapter is all about how **not** to end up at the side of the road, jelly-legged, screaming, 'Give me sugar NOW.'

Cycling is a strenuous cardiovascular exercise. You burn lots of fuel when you're cycling, even more when you're carrying luggage; the received wisdom is about 40 calories per mile if riding at about 14-15 miles per hour. This figure is the least you need to replace if you don't want to feel miserable and tired all the time, or if you don't want to be overtaken by the sudden refusal of your legs to move.

July 2008. I'm leaning over my handlebars at the side of a Yorkshire lane, holding onto the cowhorn grips with trembling fingers that don't quite feel as if they belong to me. I'm trying to keep my bike upright with legs that feel horribly empty and wobbly, as if my calves have changed into two huge, hungry stomachs with empty, gaping mouths. My thighs feel like jelly. The brambly verge looks hallucinatorily inviting. I know that the campsite is less than two miles away but all I can think is 'My legs are hungry,' and I know I can't go another inch without food. This is not my brain talking; my brain gave up some time ago. It is what my body is saying, very loudly.

I am having a bonk.

'Bonking' is the term that athletes, particularly cyclists, apply to a hypoglycaemic episode. This occurs when the easily available sugars in the form of glycogen, which muscles store and burn to provide them with energy, have all been used up. If there are no simple sugars in the blood, the muscles will turn in on themselves. It is a horrible sensation and can have dangerous side effects, with irritability and poor judgement preceding the physical symptoms of weakness, confusion and ultimately unconsciousness.

In my case, my first bonk classically exhibited the mental, emotional and physical symptoms.

Fortunately, we were not entirely unprepared. My wobbly happened almost exactly an hour and a half after we set out, which is the classic time it takes for a bonk to set in. I inhaled half of a seed-stuffed, honey-laden cereal bar and ate the rest in two bites. We waited in silence. The weakness faded slowly, until I felt able to get back on the bike. Rationality returned with strength, and I was able to apologise for my bonk-induced shouting.

How muscles work

Muscles burn glucose for energy. The body doesn't store raw glucose; it makes it from breaking down other substances: fats, proteins and complex carbohydrates. Muscles store glucose for their immediate needs in the form of glycogen, with enough stored at any one time for about ninety minutes of moderately intense exercise. The trouble starts when you keep exercising after this ninety minutes. The ongoing process of making glycogen – from stored fats, for example – is too slow to keep up with the demands of the working muscles, so they look to the food you have most recently eaten and that is still being processed by your body and carried around in your blood. This is why it is important to eat carbohydrates; they can be broken down to glycogen swiftly and transported to the muscles that need it, so they can fall upon it and convert it to energy. Keeping topped up with foods that are easily converted to glycogen will keep the bonk at bay.

What should you eat?

In order to enjoy your days in the saddle, you need a mixture of foods that will release glucose quickly and those that will release it more slowly over time. A useful guide to this is the Glycaemic Index (GI). Arising from research into diabetes, the glycaemic index is a system that ranks foods according to how easily they are converted to glycogen. The higher the food is on the index, the easier it is broken down to glycogen. Pure glucose is 100 on the index.

High GI foods, ranking over 80 on the index, include things like white bread, most breakfast cereals, mashed potatoes, honey, sweet biscuits, crackers and couscous. Mid-high GI foods, in the 60s and 70s, include some muesli bars, white rice and dried fruit like raisins. Mid-low GI food includes whole-wheat pasta and rice, oats and oat-based products and apricots. Low GI foods include leafy vegetables, pearl barley and pulses such as chickpeas and lentils.

For riding, a good approach is to eat foods with a middle to low GI before you ride, which will release their glucose to the muscles slowly, with mid to high GI foods as regular snacks. After your ride, you will need carbohydrates to replace those you have used up, so that your body has time to digest them and ensure that you'll will be starting off again in the morning with muscles with a full complement of glycogen, as well as plenty of easily-convertible carbohydrates floating around in your blood.

Of course, you need protein to repair the muscle cells damaged during exercise, and some fats as well. But if you keep in mind that you need a good mix of GI foods and build out your meals and snacks around that, you should avoid any nasty occurrences.

One important point to note is that it is possible to have a full stomach and still experience the bonk if the food you are full of does not contain enough accessible sugars that your muscles can quickly use. It's most unpleasant when you don't want to eat any more but you know that you must.

How often should you eat?

It's generally agreed that you should eat within the first forty-five minutes and every half-hour after that. It might sound crazy to say you need to practise eating while riding, but you should. It doesn't come naturally. 'Eat before you're hungry, drink before you're thirsty' is old hands' advice that makes a lot of sense and will help to avoid horrible experiences. With practice you'll learn what feels right for you, how often and how many mouthfuls of what kind of food you need to keep you going.

How often should you drink?

Our bodies are sensitive to even mild fluctuations in the volume of water in our tissues, organs and blood (50-60%). Neglecting to drink for even a few hours will have noticeable effects, as water removed from the body in the form of urine, sweat and evaporation (from the moist surfaces of the eyes, nose and lips) is not replaced. Even mild dehydration (1-2% of your body weight) will make you feel a bit under the weather. Dizziness, lethargy and headaches can result if even mild dehydration continues, as the effects are cumulative.

Getting into the habit of taking regular sips from your water bottle will prevent you getting dehydrated, and let you get on with the business of enjoying your cycle tour.

On the subject of water bottles, we each carry at least two 750 ml capacity bidons. Bear in mind that a bite valve can be unhygienic unless it has a cover (think about what your wheels roll through sometimes...) We also carry a bladder-style water carrier, and often litre bottles strapped on top of the back panniers as well.

What should you drink?

Personally, I prefer just to drink water. If I get bored with water, I'll buy a bottle of cordial and use that. Adi and I also enjoy drinking good fruit juices, which are a good source of vitamins as well as naturally occurring sugars. We often dilute these.

If I feel I need an extra hit – during an afternoon slump, for example, with an ominous hill looming — I might buy a Lucozade or something similar, for an injection of sugars and an energy boost. However, I try to avoid getting into situations where I'm tempted to do this, as sugary drinks can leave you with a crash once your body has pounced on all the sugars. This applies to purely sugary foods also, for example glucose lozenges. If you do use these, try to make sure that you've already eaten some low GI foods, that will be slowly releasing sugars over time. This will help to cushion the crash after eating or drinking something high in sugars.

Neither of us is fond of sports drinks. We didn't see anything like the shelf space devoted to sports drinks now common in most UK supermarkets in Italian, French or Spanish shops. In my opinion, that's all to the good. Much is made on sports drink packaging of replacing electrolytes that are lost through sweat, which is undoubtedly important. However, we generally manage by drinking plenty of water, eating bananas (high in potassium and other electrolytes), up-ping the amount of salt we put in our sandwiches and dinner, and eating as broad a variety of fruit as we can.

You can go much deeper into sports nutrition if you wish, but the aim of this book is to encourage you to get out and try cycle touring. The advice above should help you to avoid jelly-legged experiences.

Our diet on tour

We differ from a lot of cycle tourers that we've met in that we eat enormous breakfasts. Enormous. We pare them down if we're not intending to ride very far, but experience has taught us that a break-fast including lots of low-GI carbohydrates and a good dose of pro-tein will get us cheerfully through most of the morning.

Obviously your tastes will differ, but this should give an idea of how much food and how frequently we eat while riding in two differ-ent climates. We both lose weight every time, but that's incidental; losing weight is not the point of the cycling diet below.

A typical day in the south of France

Breakfast

Wholegrain baguette, with as many seeds and cereals as possible, with liberal dollops of honey. If we have a series of taxing days com-ing up we try to pick up a carton of eggs (not the easiest of foods to carry on a bike) and make a sort of scrambled egg baguette sandwich. Washed down with Earl Grey tea (me) and weapons-grade perco-lated coffee (Adi), and plenty of water before we start riding.

Morning snacks on the road

Apples have a surprisingly low GI, giving a long, slow release of sugar into your bloodstream, though they can get bruised in the bar bag. We both like to keep a banana handy, maybe with a small packet of oatcakes. Oats are a wonderful foodstuff for keeping you going steadily. I also like to keep a bit of a bread roll or baguette handy for occasional top-up bites.

Lunch

Usually a baguette filled with cheese and apple or cheese and tomato. I like to finish with an extra apple; Adi prefers to finish with an orange. The size of our lunch will depend upon whether we are continuing on our ride or taking a few hours off the bike to go exploring on foot; if we are carrying on I prefer to have a smaller lunch, and eat more small snacks – just a mouthful at a time, every 20-30 minutes – during the afternoon.

Afternoon snacks

This will be any combination of bites of baguette with dollops of honey, occasional apples and oatcakes.

Dinner

Pasta or couscous, occasionally potatoes, with a sauce based on onion, tomato and whatever vegetables we could buy that day – aubergine, peppers, mangetout, green beans, carrots – bulked out with chickpeas or lentils for protein. An inevitable bottle of wine and, most importantly, chocolate.

France, incidentally, is a wonderful country for the wandering self-caterer, as all but the tiniest of villages has its market, and fresh fruit and vegetables are by and large delicious and inexpensive. We both stick to a vegetarian diet, though Adi sometimes eats fish when we eat out, and it was perfect for us. The only thing you have to watch out for is the Monday closing that is still very widespread in rural areas. This usually resulted in us having a panic-buy on Saturday afternoon to make sure that we could survive until Tuesday morning if we had to.

The older I get the harder I find it to finish dinner without something sweet, and when touring it's an indispensable treat at the end of the day. A couple of squares of good quality, dark, nutty chocolate makes my evening. (See the chapter on 'Luxuries'.)

A typical day in Scotland and northern England

Our diet on the road tends to be a bit different on cycling tours closer to home, reflecting what is available. In Scottish islands the shops are few and far between, though normally, when you find them, stuffed with everything that an islander and traveller could want. Quite often, we found, they don't look like shops; one day, Adi spotted one, the only clues a few parked cars outside what looked like a shed and a couple of people emerging with shopping bags. 'I just want to see what they've got,' he said, an hour later (if there is a bargain to be had, my partner will find it).

This scarcity of shops means that if you are looking for fresh fruit and vegetables, you need to be very on-the-ball or be stalking a local. They all know which days of the week the fruit and vegetables arrive on the ferry for restocking (I'm sure it can't be daily) and they've cleaned it out by ten in the morning. Many were the times we pulled up to a shop in the early afternoon, seeking ingredients for the evening meal, to be left once again disconsolately regarding an elderly onion and a rock-hard orange. After two weeks on the outer Hebrides a few years ago we felt so starved of fresh fruit that when we got back to Portree on Skye we were almost overwhelmed with the choice on offer in the supermarket. I can still taste the melon we savaged in the main square.

Potato cakes are our favourite Scottish breakfast; mid-GI potatoes and high-GI flour are a great booster in the morning. Dinner is usually based on pasta – spaghetti for its packability – and whatever sauces we can buy along the way. We always keep at least one emergency meal in reserve, even if it's as dull as plain pasta with olive oil and black pepper.

Another consequence of the relative dearth of fresh fruit and vegetables in the Scottish islands was that we ate in restaurants quite often; in fact we ended up spending a fortune, as it was the only way we could be sure we'd get our vitamins, and we really, really felt as if we needed them.

A great book that campers of any sort should read is *Moveable Feasts* by Amy-Jane Beer and Roy Halpin. They include a section with a simple but clear description of what happens as your body converts food into fuel for your muscles, and a table showing the typical calorie-consumption per hour of various outdoor activities. The recipe section is stuffed with good, portable meal ideas.

You won't be surprised by now if I emphasise that fretting about food should not keep you from trying out an overnight cycling trip, or a weekend, or a week, starting RIGHT NOW! However, time spent paying a little attention to your food – your fuel – will repay you by making things easier on your body. Staying well fed and watered can be the difference between a challenging experience – a closed campsite at the end of the day with the next one ten miles away over two hills, for example – and a downright horrible one.

CHAPTER 5

Panniers & Other Luggage

In this chapter I'll outline the various ways you can carry what you've decided to bring, starting with the type of luggage you can use and going on to some advice on how to pack it sensibly.

Guess what I'm going to say first.

If all you have is a rucksack, you can try cycle touring. Do not be put off because you don't have shiny waterproof baggage hanging from your rack. Use a day bag for a few changes of clothes or strap a sports bag to the rear rack. Remember the man riding around the coast of Devon? The main thing is to try it.

That said, you'll be astonished at just how much you can carry on a bicycle when you need to. The downside of this, of course, is that you may be tempted to carry too much. I'll come back to this later.

The range of cycling-specific luggage on offer now is enormous, and many an afternoon when you should really be doing something else can be whiled away flicking through the catalogues that some-times come with cycling magazines, or browsing the outdoor shops on the internet. Here are a few things to bear in mind before parting with your cash.

The amount of luggage you need will be dictated by:

1. Whether or not you will be camping.

2. How long you plan to be on the road.

I put them in this order because if you're not camping there's a load of kit you can forget about. You really only need your clothes, toiletries and those luxuries that it would be silly to do without (more on luxuries later). Whether camping or not, the duration of the trip doesn't make an enormous amount of difference to what you need to bring. For long trips we bring a wider range of clothes, including wet-weather gear, some extra guide books and slightly expanded medical and tool kits. None of these take up large amounts of space.

If you're travelling on a normal bike, the luggage options, stripped of all fancy detail, come down to:

1. A bar bag – not too large or heavy.

2. Two large rear panniers.

3. Smaller front panniers.

4. Small saddle and under-bar bags.

5. Extra bags on the rear rack.

6. Trailer, instead of or in addition to panniers.

I'm sure you've seen some original variations on this set-up: long narrow bags strapped under the cross-bar, large round bags facing front, strapped to the tube under the handlebars, but at the beginning it's easier to keep to the basics above. The four-pannier arrangement is by far the most popular and enduring among cycle tourers. I haven't felt any need to deviate from it yet.

Before going on to see whether you actually need all of these or not, some points to consider when borrowing or buying panniers or other assorted luggage include:

1. Waterproofing. Absolutely essential.

2. Capacity.

3. Extra pockets, and how easy it is to access them.

4. Ease of attachment to the bicycle. This sounds small, but fixings differ hugely in design.

5. Reflective markings – useful for shady roads and dull weather conditions.

Let's look at some of these in more detail.

1. Waterproofing

Your kit *must* stay dry. Many panniers are made from waterproof material, such as the Ortlieb range, with a roll-down top so that water can't penetrate anywhere through the opening. I use these on the front, with a large pair of Altura panniers on the rear. I've had them for years and they've endured plenty of rain (and I'm including Scottish rain here). The Alturas have a pull-down cover over an inner lining. The outer material does take on some water during prolonged downpours, and the outer pockets do sometimes get damp, but even in the worst weather I've only ever found the faintest hint of dampness in items at the very top of the pannier, just where the inner lining closes. This is easily countered with sensible packing.

If you don't have panniers yet, or don't have waterproof ones, improvise. Dry bags come in all shapes and sizes. Plastic bags can be pressed into service to keep essentials dry as a bone. Some panniers come with extra waterproof coverings. My Arkel bar bag's inner lining is waterproof, so while the outer can get irritatingly sodden the contents are protected. It hasn't failed me in three seasons. Adi's Agu comes with a detachable hi-visibility waterproof cover.

2. Capacity

Adi and I started off using a bar bag, two rear panniers and a couple of extra dry bags containing the tent (which Adi always carries, although I do usually take the pegs) and anything that we couldn't fit into the panniers — usually shoes, extra water and other awkward items. We managed for a couple of years until we started taking longer trips, and the pile of small bags sitting across the panniers behind the saddle was growing. We decided to move up to the four-pannier arrangement.

Adi already had Ortlieb rear panniers and no complaints, so we both went for Ortliebs this time. Front panniers meant acquiring front racks. I bought a Tubus front rack from eBay; all the reviews I'd read said they were the best, plus they are made of steel and therefore weldable. Fitting them to my fork was a bit of a pain, but finally there they were. After some messing about with packing, deciding where things would go, we went off on a ride across northern England with a friend.

It was wonderful. No more the feeling of losing all momentum the minute the gradient changed from horizontal to 1%. No more the sensation that a nasty little homunculus was gripping my seat post and attempting to haul me backwards down each hill. With the weight now distributed more evenly between the four panniers I maintained more momentum, occasionally startling Adi when he turned around expecting me to be in my usual position half a hill behind him. Previously, I had been living in the bottom three gears, but when I moved up to four panniers the more even weight distribution meant my stubbornness and stamina had more of a chance against the gradients. I'll never go back to two panniers again.

Other tourers we've met disagree, citing the dangers of carrying too much. And it is a very real danger. Two days into that first four-pannier trip I found myself wondering if I could sneak away from the lads to find a post office and post a large bundle of unnecessary items back home. (A pair of poi. What was I thinking?) Yes, it was more evenly distributed, but it was still heavy. As a result of that episode I've become much more disciplined with my packing.

The most popular alternative luggage system is a bike trailer. I've never used one for touring but I did use one for a few months for a delivery job with the sustainable transport charity Sustrans. The little milk-crate-on-wheels I was issued with was far less sophisticated than others I've seen on the road. Trailers can be combined with panniers, of course, though I can't imagine why anyone would want to; it's hard enough to park a laden bike sometimes. Also, if you do the pannier-plus-trailer thing, the temptation to bring too much must be almost overwhelming. I'd stick to one or the other.

I've met people who swear by trailers. The mass is low down behind you and once you start rolling you're not really aware of it. The handling feels more normal without the heaviness of laden forks, or the imminent uncontrolled wheelie sensation you get sometimes when climbing a steep hill with two heavy rear panniers. However, you do have to be careful when cornering and particularly when descending. It's easy to forget about the trailer on a joyful descent until you see, out of the corner of your eye, your luggage rise into the air after a bump in the tarmac. Alarming enough with a little box of leaflets; even more alarming if it holds all your belongings and your cat (yes, I have met people cycle touring with their cat).

As ever, my advice is to use what you have. Four panniers will help you distribute the weight, but two will do. A rucksack will do. Just try it.

---

3. Extra pockets.

These are great for those small items that you need often but not frequently enough to keep in your bar bag, such as spare money, keys, tyre levers, phone chargers, lock – you'll have your own list. These pockets come into their own if you eschew a bar bag altogether, as I sometimes do when going for short trips not too far home. Webbed pockets might be right inside the pannier, as is the case with our Ortliebs, or outside the main compartment, as in my Alturas. You'll need to remember exactly where you've stowed your items, though.

4. Attachments.

A tiny point, but make sure you actually can get the pannier or bar bag on and off the bike easily. I love my Arkel bar bag but I hate the fixing arrangement: aluminium rails on the back of the bar bag slide onto the supporting arms fixed to the handlebars. I regularly have to apply lip balm to the rails to keep it working smoothly. The Ortlieb and Altura panniers use different attachment systems but both are easy to lift on and lift off the bike. You don't want to be wrestling with your panniers in the rain at your campsite. I have been there. Not fun.

It's worth making sure the attachments are easily fixable if they break, either with supplied spare parts or with innovative use of bungee cord, tie straps or gaffer tape. Like all small things, if something goes wrong with them it can cause awkwardness out of all proportion to the size of the part. After an encounter with a pothole one summer I was forced to bodge a rear pannier on with bungee cord each morning, and it regularly reduced me to rage.

Handling the bike when laden

It's worth practising with your bike laden, whatever style of loading you choose, before you go out onto the road. Even ten or fifteen minutes will help; it doesn't take long to get used to, but it will feel odd. Tight turns are more exciting, bunny-hopping is possible but much more ouch-inducing. Braking will require more of an appointment-making mindset than usual.

If you just use two rear panniers, with all the weight at the back, the forks will feel very light and you'll feel the weight strongly when going up hills. Front panniers and a bar bag both affect the steering.

As noted above, with a trailer the bike handles much more like a bike. Hills are harder and slower, but there isn't quite the same disconcerting effect of gravity getting personal with you as there is when all your luggage is on the rear rack. In spite of that, I can't see myself ever going touring with one, mainly because I didn't enjoy going down hills with it, and also because (perhaps this is just me) it is too easy to forget that you are pulling a trailer when you can't see it. You can never forget that you are laden with panniers.

What are you going to put in your panniers?

I'll address this in the following chapters, but before that I want to refer back to that first over-laden ride with four panniers. Getting excited about the extra capacity and bringing far too much had one positive outcome. We finished in Robin Hood's Bay on the North Sea coast where our campervan, full of clean clothes and food and drink, was waiting for us. As we trundled up to it and congratulated ourselves I did one of the most sensible things I've ever done in my life. 'Off you go,' I said to Adi. 'I'm going to have a cup of tea.' So I did, on the comfy camping chair tucked out of the breeze, with a notebook on my lap, mug of tea in one hand and pen in the other. I went through my bar bag, panniers and extra bags, and listed every single item I had brought, whether or not I'd used it, and if so, how often. (Example: Poi. Used once, out of pure stubbornness, when waiting for Jim to get back having called a taxi to the middle of no-where where his chain had broken – a story in itself. Little sleeveless cotton hippy top with lace-up back: NONE. Fleece: every night.)

It was mortifying. I didn't actually weigh the unused and little-used items but the sheer quantity was embarrassing enough. Ever since, I've used that list as a template to sort out the 'Would be handy if...' from the 'Would be in deep trouble without...' I highly recommend that you do the same!

CHAPTER 6

Where To Stay

This comes down entirely to personal choice. I am a dyed-in-the-wool camper, but please, please don't think that cycle touring precludes luxury. You can afford hotels every night? Good for you! Get on a bike and ride to them. You'll enjoy them all the more for having ridden there with a few clothes and essentials on your bike. I'm looking forward to luxury cycle touring when I can afford it and if I ever fall out with camping. There are a few upsides to the different kinds of accommodation, outlined briefly below.

Most of my own cycle touring experiences have been under canvas, but I've stayed in pensions in Spain, gîtes in France, hostels, guest houses and, once, a motorway hotel.

Before going into the different kinds of accommodation, I'd like to make it clear that I am not a total tightwad. I just love to camp, and, for me, inexpensive accommodation means more money for a longer holiday, time for more miles on the bike, more unknown corners to ride around, more unknown vistas awaiting my greedy eyes. Your priorities may be different: fewer days out but more luxurious accommodation. You don't have to do it any particular way. Balance it your way.

Camping

Advantages

Almost certainly the cheapest option, although if you're travelling abroad do research the country where you are going. Indoor options may be just as affordable. In the UK, it is usually by far the cheapest option, even more so if you can wild camp. Wild camping can considerably bring down your accommodation costs, freeing up your budget for a longer holiday, visiting more museums or more luxurious meals.

Wild camping is permitted in Scotland, provided you keep to the Scottish Outdoor Access Code, which basically means be considerate and don't leave any traces of your presence – litter, fire or toilet waste. It is also permitted in some parts of the National Parks in England and Wales, but you must seek and get the landowner's consent; guidelines are available at the National Parks website. Be aware though that in England and Wales, permissible wild camping areas are unlikely to be accessible from roads or tracks.

Remember that some campsites may only open in high season, so check beforehand for the region you'll be travelling in.

Disadvantages

Camping can be miserable if the weather gets bad and stays bad. Lying awake knowing that you'll have no way of drying the tent if you have to pack it away wet is no way to spend a night. I've been there, on my knees inside a still damp inner tent beside a mountain of sodden toilet roll that looks like a dead sheep, desperately trying to dry it while the rain continues to hammer down.

Weather can force you to change your plans. One way we deal with continuous rain is to stop an extra night or two on a campsite, if we can afford the time, and go for day rides instead. Unless dreadfully unlucky, you are bound to get at least a brief break where you can put the tent away more or less dry after a couple of days. However, another way to deal with rain is to pedal on through it; you might as well! How else are you going to experience the bliss of riding along deserted rainy lanes and being in just the right spot to get the first ray of sunshine of the day on the back of your droplet-coated calves?

Resources

Guidebooks such as Rough Guides and Lonely Planet are generally reliable, though not exhaustive. In the Western Isles in Scotland, we once picked up a leaflet in a pub that listed public showers and managed wild-camp spots the length of the archipelago. Up-to-date Ordnance Survey Outdoor Leisure maps usually indicate campsites. Useful websites include www.UKcampsite.co.uk and www.CoolCamping.co.uk, which covers some European countries as well as the UK and Ireland. For the USA and Canada, www.USCampgrounds.info lists 13,000 public campsites.

I go into types of tent in the chapter on Tent And Accessories.

Hostels

Advantages

Wonderfully inexpensive, and dotted around all the UK and Europe, including in some towns and cities. For not much more than the cost of a luxury campsite pitch, you'll be under cover, out of the rain, often with the chance of drying out sodden kit.

Disadvantages

Hostel facilities vary widely from basic to good guest house standard. Don't expect too much and you'll be pleasantly surprised. Some may not have private rooms, which for me is decidedly off-putting; I am not a dormitory-minded person. We once camped in the garden of a hostel on Berneray, one of the Western Isles, paying a small fee to do so and to have access to the showers and kitchen as a predicted storm gathered over the islands. I spoke to an elderly lady who was walking the islands, clearly a very experienced hosteller, who considered sleeping in a tent to be far too hardcore; I hold exactly the same opinion of sleeping in a roomful of strangers.

Resources

You don't have to be particularly youthful to join the Youth Hostelling Association, which is a member of Hostelling International. Most of the time you have to be a member, but you can usually join on arrival. There are also many independent hostels throughout the UK and Ireland, listed on the Independent Hostel Guide website and the Scottish Independent Hostel Association's website.

In France, the gîte d'etape occupies a similar niche to hostels in the UK. Unlike the normal gite, which is basically a self-catering cottage, gîtes d'etape are geared towards those who will be moving on after a night or two. They are frequently off the beaten track.

Guest houses, bed & breakfasts and hotels

Advantages

Not being vulnerable to the vagaries of the weather is the biggest one; being able to dry your clothes comes a close second. Even if you're mainly taking the budget option, if you're out for a long time you might consider planning a couple of hotel stops as treats. Having a shower in your room or down the hall rather than across a field, and being able to dry yourself without the complications of a wet cubicle with no shower curtain, are luxuries almost beyond price. (I could write reams on my obsessive-compulsive-camping-shower drying rituals.)

Loving camping as we do, all our hotel or pension stopovers have been of the result of necessity, having found (at eleven o'clock at night in June) that the campsite in Orléans doesn't open until July, for example, or, having cycled seventy-five miles through hilly north Spain, that the campsite is another five miles too far.

Disadvantages

Cost. However, the advantages above may be worth it to you. This may also be less flexible than camping or hostelling, as you may need to book ahead to ensure you'll have a room.

Whatever you decide in the end, remember to do whatever you'll enjoy the most. Don't compare yourself to others. There's no need to feel as if you're not a proper cycle tourer if you're staying in a lovely hotel. Of course you are. You cycled there, didn't you?

CHAPTER 7

To Plan Or Not To Plan Your Route

There is no right or wrong way to plan a trip. Expeditions of months will necessitate some planning which is beyond the scope of this book, but making it up as you go along is just as valid an option. If you start at the south of France and know that your ferry is booked from Saint-Malo on a certain date, then you have a direction and a deadline. We did this in 2012, knowing in advance that we would probably take a train through the flatter regions between Périgord and the Loire. Beyond that, we made it up.

Here are some things you might want to consider when deciding whether you're going to plot and plan or just go by the seat of your pants.

Time available

Planning in detail can be very helpful if all you've got is a few days, and want to fill them rather than waste time at crossroads deciding which way to go. On our very first tour, a ride across northern England from the Cumbrian coast on the west to Robin Hood's Bay in the east, Adi made reservations at each of the campsites in advance, and mapped out the route in great detail, marking it out on our Ordnance Survey maps. The advantage was that we didn't have to think about where we were going, or make any decisions en route; all we had to do was make sure we were on course.

Motivation

Whatever the length of your proposed trip, having planned your route can be a great motivator to keep going and get to your planned stops.

Peace of mind

Booking accommodation means that you definitely have some-where to stay. It hasn't happened to us often, but we have pulled up in villages or at campsites where we didn't feel comfortable. Once in Scotland we arrived in a village where, according to three separate sources – I forget which, Adi had done all that – there was a campsite. We asked a cheerful lad who was weeding his flower beds. 'Oh, you mean the one old Ray used to have?' On our first trip across England, we had somewhere to aim for and were able to phone to let the camp-site owner know on the first two evenings that we were going to be a bit late. The weather was so horrible that if we hadn't booked the sites, we'd probably have given up early, in which case we'd have had to ride around trying to find somewhere, or to spend time phoning around possibilities, choosing a site and then trying to find it. As it was, we carried on into the rain, and I am trying not to sound too pink and fluffy here, but there were gorgeous moments during the downpours: riding around a bend and meeting a very large man in a very small car as we rounded the top of Ullswater; finally eating, having picked our way through the farmyard for a shower, in the awning of the tent at ten at night, the most delicious dinner. Yes, planning can be great for short time and long-distance rides.

Time of year and destination

Some places are permanent honeypots; some get unbelievably busy in the high season. It's not just towns and cities that get busy either; try cycling round the ring of Kerry with coach after coach belching exhaust fumes at you, or around the remote but lovely Gorges of Verdon in Provence in the tourist season when the tiny precipitous cliff-hugging road is clogged with cars. If you don't have a choice but to go in high season, it will probably be advisable to book at least some of your accommodation. Check the advice in the country or regional travel guides.

CHAPTER 8

Tools and Repair Kits

My attitude to an emergency tool kit is minimalist. At home and on a normal ride, it can be as simple as a £5 note, a credit card and a mobile phone.

Weight is the biggest consideration with your tool kit. You'll need to consider carefully how often you're likely to use the heavier items, and if you'll really be that far from somewhere where you'll be able to borrow or buy what you need. We once brought an adjustable spanner to France with us. We used it to put the pedals back on the bikes after the train journey to Avignon. That was its only function. The task took five minutes and then Adi had to carry the spanner around France for two months. Now our touring pedals can be re-moved and replaced with a chunky 8 mm hex key, so we don't even need the spanner for that.

The length of your trip will increase the size of your repair kit but there isn't a lot of difference between what you might carry for a week and what you'd bring for a couple of months.

On lone overnight trips and on short trips with Adi (a week or so) my toolkit consists of:

- Lock
- Spare inner tube

- Tyre levers
- Puncture repair kit
- Multi-tool with hex keys from 2 mm to 8 mm, flat-head and cross-pointed screwdrivers and a star key
- Emergency credit card
- Mobile phone

At this point I have to make a confession. Adi carries the tool kit. It lives in one of his front panniers and I have only a hazy idea what's in it. I've just been to ask him and he formally asks that he be credited as Technical Consultant.

Before listing the tools, it's worth mentioning that if there are two or more of you travelling together, it's very handy if the key components are the same style for all of the bikes – the same wheel and tyre sizes, the same size inner tube and valve type, the same type of brakes and brake pads, and so on. You can then pool your tools and spares and carry less per person than you would have taken individually.

Bike-specific tools

This is what I, I mean Adi, carries in the way of tools for anything over a couple of weeks. This is for two people cycle touring together.

- Two gear cables
- Two brake cables
- Set of brake blocks for each bike
- At least one inner tube each – I bring two
- Puncture repair kit with quick acting adhesive squares and fine sandpaper
- Tyre levers – at least two, preferably three

• Multi-tool with a set of hex keys. Most bolts on your bike will require a 3-6 mm hexagonal key, but it's worth taking the time to check all the little bolt heads to make sure you have a key that will undo each of them. My stand, for instance, takes an 8 mm hex key to tighten it, and a 2 mm key to adjust its length. Make sure that you have a screwdriver head compatible with the tiny screws that adjust the end stops on the derailleurs.

• Small bottle of chain oil.

• Couple of pairs of latex disposable gloves – handy if you need to dismantle and rebuild the bike if travelling by train or air.

General purpose tools and repair kit

• A small roll of quality gaffer tape. This tape is expensive, and usually comes in big rolls. Spool a good length of it off around something smaller, like the stub of a pencil.

• A small selection of threaded nuts and bolts compatible with those on your pannier racks. These will usually be size M6, but check. Most of our few misadventures have involved snapping or shearing of pannier and rack related hardware. There's no need to go over the top, a couple will do.

• A general purpose multi-tool in addition to the bike-specific one. We have an imitation Leatherman device which opens out into a pair of pliers, with other smaller tools tucked into the arms. It's light and small.

• Tie-straps, good quality, in a selection of sizes. They are sold according to width. Adi brings a couple in each size, up to 8 mm wide. The biggest are sturdy enough to hold almost any part of the bike on in case something snaps; a tie strap held the rear rack to Adi's bike when one of its struts expired on a patchwork road surface. Good tie-straps and gaffer tape will hold most of a bike together until you reach a store or a bike mechanic.

•   Bungee cords, various sizes and lengths. We usually use these for holding extras onto the rear racks or the top of the panniers, and occasionally for holding broken bits together. They come with a variety of hook types. I used a bungee cord to hold one of my rear panniers on for two weeks when the attachment broke – not ideal, but it worked.

Tent pole repair kit. This is a small aluminium sleeve that fits over the broken ends of the snapped pole. Most mid- to high-end tents will come supplied with one, but if you're buying second-hand, check for the repair kit and buy one if not included.

CHAPTER 9

Camping Equipment

learly, you can skip this if you're not planning to camp, but I do seriously urge you to try it. If it seems a bit too daunting on your first go, then stay in a hostel, a hotel, somewhere comfortable, but GO! But please don't discount camping forever.

If you fully intend to camp, great. Here's my advice.

Tent

I'll start with my usual refrain: don't let the lack of a super-light, technical tent stop you from having a go. It doesn't need to be clever: you need to be able to put it up and put it down, have just enough knowledge to know where not to pitch it, and it should keep you dry at night. Don't worry about the weight for now if it's terribly heavy; if it's your first time cycle touring then it is an excuse to go a little more slowly, to take your time a bit more and to eat a bit more cake. I once met a couple going round the UK in a cheap and heavy little dome tent. It did the job, got them out on the road. Yours will too.

If you're at the stage where you're thinking of investing in one that you'd like to use for many tours in the future, I'd first recommend talking to any other cycle tourers you bump into on your first few exploratory trips. Shape is largely a matter of personal preference, but some styles seem to suit cycle touring more particularly. I go through some of the more common shapes below.

Tunnel

When we first started we bought a Vango Spirit 300+, a tunnel tent intended for three friendly people, even though there are only two of us. We wanted to be comfortable inside it (most of our intended travels were to be in northern England and Scotland and we are realists about weather), we wanted to be able to pull the bikes right undercover if we felt we needed to and we wanted to be able to cook in the doorway if necessary. We wanted space in the awning for all our luggage (eight panniers, two bar bags, tent-bag and extras bag), plus a little floor area where we'd be able to divest ourselves of wet outer layers (again being realistic about the weather) without soaking the inner or brushing up unintentionally against a partner who had just managed to dress in dry, cosy clothes. There is no sensation yuckier than your clean, warm, dry clothes coming into contact with a wet pair of leggings. This tent saw us through three three-week tours in Scotland, at least three coast-to-coast rides in northern England, numerous short trips in north Wales and south-west Ireland, nine weeks in France and other non-cycling camping trips, before the zips gave up and the waterproofing became suspect, particularly in the groundsheet.

I've just checked the tent's description, which says it weighs 3.25 kg. That tent kept us and all of our belongings as dry as possible even on tours where it rained every day.

One consideration with tunnel tents is that you have to make sure that you are pitched into the wind, which can leave you at a disadvantage in changeable weather. Our worst experience was having a tent-pole snap in our Vango when the wind, which had been changing all day and had already forced us to move the tent around once, changed in the middle of the night. We went to sleep, having done the best we could. In the night, naturally enough, the wind veered 90°, banging at us side on. The tent didn't breach though; it was designed well enough so that the snap occurred on the leeward side. It was a bit of a carry-on sorting it all out, as it was still raining – getting everything out, collapsing the tent, fixing it, re-erecting it, putting wet panniers back in having rolled back the footprint in an effort to keep at least a part of it dry, setting up the bedding again. Still, it was one way to start a 40th birthday.

Another thing that puts some people off tunnel tents is the number of pegs required, which means it takes longer to erect (which is irritating in wind and rain) and difficult or impossible to peg out fully in stony or hard, sun-baked soil, which is irritating in an entirely different way. Despite this, when it became clear that our Vango was getting a bit weather-worn, we opted to stick with the tunnel tent design, this time a Hilleberg Nallo 2 GT. We chose this because it was slightly smaller and considerably lighter at 2.8 kg. We've only had two seasons with it, but we're satisfied; it is nice having that little less weight.

In short, reasons to be wary of a tunnel tent include the effects of wind, which must be considered when pitching; weight, especially with a ground sheet; and the number of pegs required to secure it. The pegs add to the weight but the real drawback becomes clear when you are trying to push a peg into baked hard ground. On the other hand, tunnel tents are very comfortable. A weighty consideration.

The following is a brief run-down of the advantages and disadvantages of other types of tent, as related to me during many conversations on campsites with mug of tea in hand just post-pitching, comparing notes with other cycle tourers.

Dome with or without awning

The biggest advantage is that dome tents are more stable in windy conditions. They also require less pegging out than a tunnel.

There is often a little more headroom in the middle of the tent than in a tunnel tent, though this does not extend to the corners.

The biggest disadvantage is space. Most only have a tiny awning, though this is extended in some styles, giving some of the advantages of the tunnel tent. Some people we've met have left some of their baggage locked outside overnight, which has obvious security disadvantages, as well as leaving it at the mercy of the weather.

Tilted dome

The same advantages apply. These are even more stable in the wind, and can be very comfortable inside, but rarely have an awning that you can use to stow all your luggage, unless you are travelling very light.

Pyramid and other shapes

I can't say anything first-hand about them, except that if all you have is a strange little tent, then at least you have a tent, which means you can try cycle touring. You don't have to have the perfect tent to start.

Bedding

Sleeping mats

We use Thermarest inflatable mats and I've forgotten how long we've had them now. We both use the shorter women's version of the Trail Lite Regular. Adi doesn't miss the extra length, and they pack down very neatly into two small cylinders. We haven't found any reason to change or upgrade.

Sleeping bags

We both use Mountain Equipment down bags. Mine is a Classic Dragon 1000 with, apparently, a comfort level of +10°C to -20°C. Adi's is a Classic 800, with a comfort range between +10°C and -17°C, which probably means that if tested he'd be shouting to come into mine 3 degrees before the cold woke me up. Both bags are getting on a bit, especially mine, and are relatively bulky to pack, but they are light and they do work. Sleeping bags with comparable thermal qualities but much less bulk are available nowadays, but as you'd expect they tend to be more costly. Ours have served us well in all conditions, from Corsica (where we brought dreadful weather with us) to the Isle of Harris.

Sleeping bag liners

If you are tempted to skimp on one item of bedding, it might be this one. My strong advice is: don't. A liner adds extra warmth, can be used on its own when it's too hot to sleep and if you have to you can get into it with smelly feet, knowing you are not sullying the sleeping bag itself. We use inexpensive silk liners that we bought from Decathlon and they're wonderful. Easy to wash and they dry in seconds. Seven weeks into a tour and you can still slip into bed be-tween fresh-smelling sheets. If you're planning a trip more than two days long, seriously, invest in these. I don't go anywhere without mine now.

Pillows

Any experienced cycle tourer reading this is either rolling their eyes or chomping at the bit to tell me about the ultimate travel pillow they've just found in a little outdoor shop in somewhere or other. We've used everything from the fleece-jumper-in-a-pillowcase to fancy inflatable pillows (my 42nd birthday present, halfway through a tour in France, was an inflatable pillow. And yes, I do spend a lot of my birthdays on the bike with a tent.) Obviously, if you're just trying it for a couple of nights for the first time, don't let the lack of a good pillow stop you from riding out into the wide blue yonder. On the other hand, if you know you'll hate it if you don't have a good night's sleep, it's worth trying different pillow options out. We're still trying to find the perfect travel pillow. If you've found it, please let me know! I broke my birthday-present-pillow in Yorkshire last summer (sat on it) and need a replacement.

Other bits

These are the random, personal items that make camping a little more comfortable and make your pitch, even if just for the night, your home. Some of these live in Adi's tool pannier because they have a practical purpose, but they are more to do with your camping pitch than with getting you out of a fix. For a night it may not matter; for a trip of a week or more, they make your stopovers individual to you and give a sense of homecoming to every new place you camp. You'll grow your own list over time.

Cotton tablecloth

We bought one in Arles in Provence a couple of years ago and now never go touring without it. Lighter than most outdoor rugs, we use it to sit on in the evening, to lie down on when the ground is too sandy or muddy or hard. If ground is wet but it's stopped raining, we lay out our spacemats (see below) and lie the tablecloth over it. We use it in place of a towel on beaches; we fold it up to make a two-person cushion for sitting on cold stone walls or metal benches. And we use it as a tablecloth when we find handy picnic benches, relishing the fact that we have the best-dressed picnic table on the road.

Spacemats

You won't find these if you search for brand names. This our pet name for our most recent cycle touring discovery, home-made sit mats, made by cutting up cheap car windscreen insulation sheets that you can buy for half nothing. Ours cost less than €3 in a Spar on Corsica. Birgit and Robert, a highly experienced pair of cycle tourers from Germany, gave us the idea. You can sit on the mats folded open, or quartered to make a thick little mat. We slide them under the footprint of our awning on rough or cold ground to give a little extra protection and insulation. We've wrapped them around food to keep it warm or cool (they kept our picnic of yoghurt, cheese and juice cool in 30°C sunshine for five hours, waiting for the Tour de France to pass). We can open them out under our tablecloth to make a comfortable and much prettier rug than anyone else's. And if we need to, we can hold them up to the sun and signal to outer space. Spacemats. See?

Extra guy ropes

Handy for making washing lines. You'll most likely want to at least air your clothes even if you don't wash them every day, and a washing line is a step up from hanging your unmentionables from your handlebars and draping them over the saddle (a fail-safe way to identify a cycle tourer at a campsite). If you don't have a handy tree you can always string the rope to your handlebars. For short trips, we normally just bring one extra guy rope, with up to three thin ropes for longer tours where we know that there will be at least one day where we take over a campsite's laundry area and wash EVERY-THING.

Dog tethering poles

No, we don't bring a dog on cycle tours. These have two uses: security and extra stability when camping on sand in windy conditions. They're about a foot in length, made of aluminium so they're not too heavy, and are shaped like a corkscrew. The idea is that you corkscrew them securely into the ground and clip your dog's lead to the top. We've used them a couple of times where we didn't feel entirely secure on the campsite, or where we were advised to by campsite staff. Adi uses them as follows: lie the bicycles down on the ground outside the tent on top of each other. Twist the tethering poles into the ground, through the frames. Loop the locks through the triangle at the top of the pole and through as many wheels and bits of frame as possible. Tie a string through the chain to your big toe – no, I made that up. But you get the idea.

They've also been very useful in Scotland, where it can be windy and where we often camp in amongst the sand dunes behind beaches; attaching the tent-end guy ropes to the tethering poles, corkscrewed well down into the ground, has kept the tent from taking flight on more than one occasion.

Camping lamps

Lighting has undergone a revolution since I started cycle touring, but as a treat, we still bring our small safety candle lantern. Head torches are a must, of course, and we have our bike lamps, but the safety candle lantern makes it feel like our spot for the evening.

CHAPTER 10

Cooking Equipment

Your cooking ancillaries will vary depending on whether you are going to be camping and cooking every night at one extreme, or eating out for every meal and staying in accommodation with roofs at the other. You can do half-and-half. I've met people who camp but always eat out, making do with a stale baguette or cereal bar for breakfast. More often, I've met people who are staying in comfortable accommodation but have brought a small stove so they can find somewhere sheltered and cook at least one meal a day, to reduce the costs of eating out. This can work very well.

We cook almost all our own meals, eating out maybe once a week. And when I say we cook, I mean Adi cooks. I chop.

Our cooking kit list looks something like this:

Equipment

- MSR Whisperlite stove and/or butane gas camping stove
- Fuel for stove
- Two light-weight windshields (different heights and design)

- Vango saucepan with lid and grab handle
- Lightweight kettle
- Two sharp Opinel knives and sharpening stone
- Corkscrew
- Small wooden spoon
- Wooden spatula
- Lightweight sporks
- Small plastic bowl
- Plastic chopping board
- Camping mugs, insulated
- Plastic glasses
- Ancient enamel plates
- Coffee percolator
- Two small lighters

Store cupboard

- Salt
- Black pepper
- Spice mix
- Herb mix
- Earl Grey tea bags
- Ground coffee

This sounds like a lot but except for the coffee percolator the individual elements are all extremely light and don't add up to much. We cut the handles of the wooden spoon and spatula. We've never found that we need a second dish to cook in; planning our meals and using the enamel plates to keep parts of the meal warm while the second part is being cooked are quite enough.

We normally start out with a couple of small empty plastic tubs, of the kind that hold miniature desserts for one. These are very good for storing spices provided the lid fits securely. The spice cupboard (Adi's domain) tends to increase in complexity with the journey.

Also in the kitchen pannier are:
- Washing up liquid in a small container
- Washing up sponge
- Tea towel
- Laundry liquid

Remember that the tea towel and sponge must be laundered regularly to avoid becoming hives of bacterial growth.

If travelling abroad, it's worth familiarising yourself with the terms for your stove's fuel in different countries, as the same or similar word can refer to completely different substances. Petrole in France, for example, is paraffin in the UK, and we found it in the cleaning sections of hardware shops. After the first few encounters we stopped telling worried-looking store assistants that we were cooking with it.

CHAPTER 11

Clothing and Toiletries

Y ou can, of course, wear technical cycling wear exclusively, but this is about cycle touring, and assumes that you'll be doing things other than cycling – exploring on foot from time to time, hopping in and out of cafés and pubs, visiting museums and heritage places of interest – so this is about clothing that will keep you warm and dry while performing a variety of functions, in a variety of places and situations.

Guess what I'm going to say.

DO NOT let the lack of super-technical padded lycra shorts stop you from trying out cycle touring. A day or two without padded shorts won't kill you. Adi and I had cycled across England twice before purchasing padded shorts.

This is not to say that purpose-made cycling gear won't help. You'll be more comfortable for longer and changes in temperature and weather won't affect you as much. In cycling, the challenge to clothing is increased because of the need to wick sweat away from your body so that you don't get wet and become cold, whilst at the same time protecting you from the effect of wind-chill. You are almost always creating your own breeze, except in circumstances where you are riding up a hill on a sunny, windless day.

You will want to bring clothes that:

- You can wear on the bike
- You can wear off the bike
- That will keep you cool when cycling
- That will keep you warm when you've stopped cycling
- That make you feel like a human being

If you already own some outdoor gear, it can be adapted to wear on the bike. My now-very-old Icebreaker merino wool t-shirts and long-sleeved tops are my staple cycling wear, since long before merino hit the cycle-clothing manufacturers as the Next Big Thing some years ago. I have yet to buy a dedicated cycling rain-jacket. I always buy a walking jacket with this dual purpose in mind, looking for a slim fit with a longer tail that comes well down over my lower back when riding. The only real disadvantage I've found is that in warm, wet weather it is easy to overheat, as the walking jacket isn't designed to cope with the amount of heat that can be generated even on a gentle ride. However, for me this is balanced by the fact that I can wear the jacket on and off the bike.

What I bring

On a two-month ride around France in 2013, my clothing pannier looked like this:

- Lycra padded shorts: two pairs. Even though I managed commuting for years without them, and our first cycle tour without them, I've got to say that padded lycra shorts do exactly what they say on the tin. They make you more comfortable, you can sit in the saddle for longer, and one of the few parts of your body not aching at the end of a long day in the saddle will be your backside. But – and I know I'm going to sound like a girl here and I don't care – I will go to my grave without inflicting the sight upon innocent bystanders. Except for super-hot days at the top of Pyrenean passes where the only other people around are other cyclists, I cover that pad with a light skirt.

- Short cycling skirt.
- Sleeveless tops: one or two. Again, these are merino wool or a light technical material, and suitable for wearing on or off the bike.
- Two merino wool t-shirts that can be worn on the bike or off it.
- One long sleeved merino, zip-neck top, for on-bike cool weather. This is what I use instead of a specific cycling jersey.
- One heavier merino wool top, zip-neck, with thumb loops. This is exclusively for non-travelling times of day, off the bike or when riding about in cool evenings, pannier-free.
- One fleece top, which acts as pillow, cosy evening jumper, or for walking trips on days off.
- One light, slightly smart t-shirt for evening and off-bike days. This is never, ever worn while cycling, and is mentally marked 'Do not sweat into this, EVER.'
- One pair of zip-off walking trousers.
- One pair of shorts.
- One dress.
- Waterproof jacket.
- Cycling sandals with cleats.
- Ordinary sandals.
- Ancient comfy pair of trainers with the mental label 'Do not get wet, EVER'.
- Reflective Sam Brown-style strap
- Sunglasses
- Baseball cap

For riding around any part of the UK or Ireland in early spring or autumn, and northern England and Scotland at any time of year, the list above changes in some details, but not significantly. There will be only one vest top, if any, no second pair of non-cycling shorts, no cycling sandals, and possibly no dress, depending upon the time of year. In addition I'll bring:

- Waterproof trousers
- Headband
- Merino wool neck-buff
- Gloves: I usually use my nephew's rugby gloves, in wet or cold weather, or a pair of silk liner gloves if it's dry and cold
- Small cycling skull-cap type hat
- Woolly hat
- Cleated SPD cycling shoes
- Kevlar overshoes
- Cycling tights
- Knee-warmers
- Arm-warmers
- Walking boots

What we wear at any given moment depends on the region we're in, the weather and the mood we're in. In summer, if we're somewhere warm like the south of France, I prefer just to wear shorts if it rains and let my legs get wet. It's easy to dry them off. In chillier climes such as northern Scotland, I'll ride in shorts with waterproof trousers over them, cinched in at the cuff. This keeps the worst of the rain off to avoid getting too chilly, while not being wrapped up enough to overheat when riding up hills, for example. On one tour in Scotland, I ended up cycling in my walking boots, for reasons I can't remember. Not ideal for the ankles, but they were waterproof, my feet were warm and dry and I could hop off the bike and go for a wander through a field to examine interesting-looking piles of stones without getting my cleats stuck full of mud.

As ever, my main point is that you don't need to spend a fortune on technical gear to get started. Work out what's going to be most useful to you, and have a go.

If you are in the mood for some shopping, there are now some companies making very nice non-sporty cycle wear from good technical fabrics, such as Minx Girl, Georgia In Dublin and Café du Cycliste. For good old lycra and sporty gear there are a million options, which I won't list: a simple Google search will bring up more padded shorts than you can browse in a lifetime.

A word about helmets and high-visibility clothing

I'll mention helmets only briefly. We wear them in countries where it is a legal requirement; we don't where it is not. This is our personal choice, and is based on experience and reading of the information available on the protection and lack of protection that helmets provide. One thing everyone agrees on, in both the pro- and anti- camps: if you are going to wear a cycling helmet, make sure it is good quality. Cheap ones are worse than useless.

If you would like more information on the debate, have a look at the Cyclists Touring Club's most recent position, or this recent piece by Chris Boardman: www.britishcycling.org.uk/article/20141103-campaigning-news-Boardman--Why-I-didn-t-wear-a-helmet-on-BBC-Breakfast-0.

The high-visibility clothing manufacturing industry has had a field day with cyclists in the UK in the last few years, with many new cyclists apparently believing that they have to be garbed in tip-to-toe yellow to ride. The truth is that eye-watering high-viz clothing on its own is only really effective for about an hour each day, in dawn and dusky conditions. It will not make you more visible at night unless it has plenty of reflective stripes on it. You will do more for your safety by making sure you have plenty of reflective strips on your bike, baggage and clothes, coupled with a set of lamps that will both make you visible and help you to see, in conditions from light mist through to full darkness.

The only high-viz items we use are a Sam Browne-style reflective belt and a pair of home-made yellow jackets with reflective stripes. Adi made these out of old high-viz work-vests, to fit over our rear offside panniers in heavy traffic. We wore them on the first day or two of our first trip in France, until we realised how much less traffic there is than in Britain, even on busy roads, and how much more respect you are given as a fellow road user over there. We very occasionally use them on busy roads in the UK at dusk.

I'll finish with three things I'd recommend if there was a gun to my head. First, padded lycra shorts or tights. Ugly, but necessary. Second, anything made from merino wool; an amazing material. And most importantly, a dress, or your favourite smart shirt and trousers: a favourite piece of clothing that you can wear to a meal out that does not look as if you have cycled fifty miles in the rain that day. A wonderful mood-booster.

CHAPTER 12

Maps, Guidebooks and Other Books

Let me repeat: you don't need any of this to start. You don't need a single book to start cycle touring. But if you are intending to try a big tour soon, this chapter might give you some ideas on what to bring. These books, maps and devices are all about finding your way around, discovering what is interesting to you about the region you are cycling in, entertaining yourself and recording your trip. You'll develop your own favourites; here's an example of what we bring.

E-reader

I can't do without my Kindle now. Phrase books, novels and travel stories in one neat package. I have now trained myself to read on my phone, so the Kindle is not as indispensable as it once was, but its battery life is far superior to that of the phone. Also, I have a great fondness for my elderly, very basic model, as it is a device purely for reading.

At least one print guide book to the region

On our last trip to France we brought the Rough Guides to Provence and Corsica (six years out of date but still useful – we left it on the ferry back to Italy for the use of any guide-less travellers on the next crossing) and some sections of the older of our editions of the Rough Guide to France, carefully scalpelled out. I admit it was quite a heavy library on the way out, but we were able to dispose of the guides in campsite bookshelves when we left the relevant regions.

You might be wondering why we bring print books rather than e-books. There are still issues with e-versions of travel guides: it's more difficult to flip back and forth between the maps and accommodation listings and so on as easily as with a print book. Travel apps are getting better all the time, but in my opinion the books still give more for their weight. And remember that with apps you either need access to wifi or to be willing to accept potentially ruinously expensive data roaming charges from your mobile phone network.

Maps

In the UK we use the relevant Ordnance Survey for the region. We've found the Landranger series, at a scale of 1:50,000, the best for cycle touring, giving enough detail for route-finding and also for exploring on foot on rest days. The Explorer series, at 1:25,000, has a level of detail that we don't usually need on the road, though they are great in areas of the country riddled with tiny lanes and bridleways. The Travel Map series (1:250,000 – about 4 miles to an inch) is great for overall regional planning, and in north-west Scotland this was fine for daily use as there are so few roads. Our copy of the Western Scotland and the Western Isles is now liberally annotated with great wild camp spots, which ferry terminals have public showers and the locations of unexpected, isolated public toilets. Other maps now sport colourful dotted lines showing our routes over the years.

The Irish Ordnance Survey's Discovery range covers the country at a scale of 1:50,000 with detail similar to that on the UK's Landranger series. Some areas of the National Parks are covered by 1:25,000 scale maps.

In France, we move between the Michelin Regional series, at 1:300,000 and the more detailed Départements series, at 1:150,000.

Satnav

We don't use a satnav but we have used the Google Maps app on our phones on occasion to get us out of fixes. We hate doing this because of data roaming charges.

Novels

Of course, I can put these on my phone now, or my Kindle, and I have done so, but I still normally contrive to find space for at least one paperback which I normally swap for another at a campsite bookshelf at some point.

Other guidebooks

Adi and I always bring guides to the region's birds, flowers and trees, because that's our thing; we work in nature conservation. These could also be included under 'luxuries', below, but I include them here to encourage you to bring such books with you if you're vacillating, wondering about the extra weight. This sort of weight is worth it. Bring that plump guide to the stately homes of southern England if that's your interest. It will add to your trip. This is meant to be fun.

Notebooks

I usually start with one but they have a habit of multiplying. I keep a journal of all our trips, squeezing in a few minutes of writing every time we pause. I encourage you to keep some sort of record of your trip, in whatever medium you like: photos, voice notes, video, text on your phone. All those moments stored ready to be enjoyed again and to encourage you to get out on another tour.

CHAPTER 13

Luxuries

These are the wonderful little things that would bring the drilling-holes-in-toothbrush brigade out into a cold sweat. Tiny chairs. Kindles. Coffee percolators. Hula hoops. A pair of sock poi. An extra pair of shoes that you only wear after your shower in the evening. A little bottle of Middleton Irish whiskey for warm nips on cold wet nights. Whatever your luxury is, you would be mental to leave it behind. As well as the effect on yourself and your companions, they can be the most tremendous icebreakers.

Looking back over old packing lists in my journals, I seem to have brought quite a lot of what could be called luxuries. I prefer to think of them as 'small things that feel like luxuries but are necessary to avoid turning into an axe murderer'. Some have been listed in earlier chapters.

- Kindle
- Camera and camera bag
- Tablecloth
- Notebook (acts as journal and random note depository)
- Two pens
- Binoculars
- Birds of Britain and Europe identification guide

- Travel guide – between one and three books
- Hula hoop (collapsible) or poi (home-made sock poi: gives an emergency pair of knee socks and a couple of tennis balls for playing throw-and-catch on beaches)
- My ancient comfy trainers that are never, ever allowed to get wet

Adi always brings his coffee percolator, which weighs nearly 800 grammes. He handed a plastic mug of coffee to a large Italian man one soggy morning in Brittany, during that awful summer of 2012 when winds blew from the west along the Loire for two weeks – exactly the length of time that we were cycling west along the valley. Straight into it. 'I am living in Marseille,' the big Italian said, gloomily looking at the forecast and a map and trying to work out how to get back to some sun. 'I am not used to this.' He paused after a sip of coffee with a smile like sunshine piercing the drizzle. He raised the mug to Adi. 'Fantastic!'

You might be all fired up with a slimming down, back-to-basics thrill, but I really, really urge you to bring something like that coffee percolator, something that will cheer you if things go against you. Because even if you're staying in hotels and eating in nice cafés, there is something basic about cycle touring. If it rains, you get wet. If there is a headwind, you have to plough on into it. If there's a thunderstorm, you have to find shelter. You have no choice but to deal with all that the weather and the road throw at you while you're out on the bike. So don't put on the hair shirt. Don't let yourself get hungry. Don't let yourself get grumpy. This is fun, but it can be hard. Reward yourself.

CHAPTER 14

Lighting and Digital

These are those items that fall between the category gaps, and are mainly to do with lighting, electronic and digital bits and pieces.

Lighting: seeing

It's possible to spend hours browsing websites and catalogues for bike lamps now. There's been a revolution in lighting in the last few years, and you can always find something to suit your budget.

Even if you do not intend to ride at night, it is worth always carrying a couple of lamps that will help you be seen if mist comes down or if you get caught out later than you expected and end up riding during dusk. I have a number of small lights wrapped around the seat post and seat stay, small flashing LEDs that ensure I'm visible from behind. Buried in my panniers are a larger rear lamp and a front lamp. It's worth spending money on the best rear lamp you can afford, as that's where the most danger is likely to come from.

We never leave home without our head torches. These are mostly for use inside the tent and for walking around at night, but they also function as extra riding lamps if the need arises.

Reflective items: being seen

Reflective stripes are especially useful on your legs, feet and pedals, which are moving and therefore catch the eye of motorists. Almost all cycle-wear will have reflective dots and strips which might not be visible until you shine a light upon them. Many makes of tyre have a reflective stripe that shows above the rim, presenting nighttime motorists with the view of two big bright circles. In the same way, most panniers have reflective shapes and emblems; the reflective triangles on our Ortliebs glow reassuringly even when cycling in dappled light under trees.

If you are like me and you like to wear ordinary clothing as well as cycle-specific clothing, you can now buy little reflective snap-on bands which can go around wrists, ankles, legs or bits of your bike. Cheeringly, colours apart from lurid yellow are now available.

Mobile phone

I usually bury mine at the bottom of a pannier, as I like to disconnect as much as possible when cycle touring. However, I'd never leave home without it, and a modern smartphone is as much of a safety item as anything else.

Bike computer

• These come in a huge range of sophistication now, from inexpensive wired models that you can buy from supermarkets to computers with every function you might ever want or need, from the basic miles per hour and average speed to telling you the air temperature (given our gift of bringing unseasonably low temperatures with us wherever we go, I never want to know this).

Computers definitely have their uses, above and beyond satisfying the inner geek. It can be instructive to see how far you have actually ridden, as opposed to what you might have estimated from your reading of the map, for example. Another useful benefit is using the computer data to compare the actual ride time logged with the time elapsed between setting off in the morning and stopping in the evening. This brought Adi and I to a realisation of how much time we spend faffing around on the journey – stopping to have a look at the map, to nip into a shop or to explore something interesting. This is fine, because it's the reason we enjoy touring. However, knowing the discrepancy has helped us to make much more sensible predictions about how far we can comfortably travel in a day, and how much we need to curtail our tendency to explore if we have a ferry we need to catch at the end of the day, for instance.

As ever, I'm going to emphasise that you don't need a computer. I deliberately don't put mine on the bike all the time; in delicate moods, a low miles-per-hour winking on the display serves only to taunt and depress.

Camera

Keeping a photographic record of your trip is a wonderful way to enjoy it over again. If you're on your own it can be more difficult to set up attractive riding-by shots, but not impossible with a small tripod, or a gorilla-pod that will grip fence posts and the like.

Chargers, cables and batteries

The advent of USB charging cables has been wonderful, turning great knots of chargers into a tiny bag of neatly coiled cables. I have a three-pin plug with USB socket that will accept the cables for my phone, camera and e-reader. We bring a two-pin converter for travelling in Europe. We also bring spare batteries for head torch, bike lamps and bike computer.

CHAPTER 15

Choosing Your Touring Companions

O r, How To Stay Friends With Your Travelling Companions.

This might sound completely obvious, but if you ride with others, you must be sure before you set off that you are expecting a similar sort of experience. Camaraderie of the road will vanish if you speed off on a hill-climbing high, heedless of the cries of a friend who just wants to stop and have a peep into that old church.

Travelling alone

Advantages
You and you alone are in charge. You can go where you like, stop where you like, change your mind where you like, take photos when you like, stop for cups of tea, or charge on as long and as fast as you like.

Disadvantages

You and you alone are in charge. Yes, it is an advantage and a disadvantage. Plus, you have to carry everything.

Travelling with a partner

Advantages

You can share heavy, essential items between you, which is no small consideration, but more importantly you can boost each other's morale when it gets hard.

Disadvantages

If you are not going to fall out you have to agree, or pretend to agree, what you are going to do and where you are going to go. You'll need to have a clear idea of the sort of cycling you each want to do – whether you are of the distance-and-challenge brigade or you want to do a join-the-dots of places to visit, or something in between.

As I said above, this might all be obvious, but it really can matter. No matter how much you adore your beloved other half, if she is eager to ride up the mountain as fast as she can while you want to stop and take photos and eat cake and admire the view and you want her there while you do so, tension will arise.

One of the reasons my partner and I get on so well is that we are quite independent in our togetherness. As long as I know that he'll wait for me at the summit, or at any potentially confusing crossroads, I'm quite happy for him to go ahead and ride at a pace that's comfortable for him up a hill rather than wait for me. This doesn't mean that he has his nose to the front wheel, not enjoying the view; it's simply that his comfortable pace is faster than mine, because, to put it plainly, he's got much bigger thighs. I wouldn't want him to ride with me all the time, as I know that it's as uncomfortable to adjust your pace to one that's unnaturally slow as it is difficult to adjust to one that's too fast. On a bend on the way up to a pass at the 2013 Tour de France in the Pyrenees, a couple of French men sitting on the corner cooking their barbecues (the memory of the Tour de France forever more will bring the smell of broiling sausages to my nostrils) looked up the hill, then back at me. 'Il ne vous attend pas?' they asked with raised eyebrows. I assured them in broken, breathy French that it was grand and he'd be waiting for me at the summit. We slow down where we like, speed up where we like, stop to take photos and then speed up to tell the other one about the funny man who spoke to us or the stoat we saw or the view from that bend just back there, that glimpse through the trees, did you see it? We enjoy sharing the over-all experience with each other while being in charge of our own pace and decisions from moment to moment.

Incidentally, this is one of the reasons we will never try a tandem together. 'But you can talk to each other on a tandem,' people have said to us. 'You can hear what the other is saying.'

Yes. You can clearly hear the other say things like 'Slow down, slow down for heaven's sake I want to stop, nobody told me there weren't any brakes on the back STOP!!!!!!'

If you are camping, sharing a tent and almost every minute of the day together, you've got to make doubly sure that you like each other from the outset and that you share roughly the same vision for your trip. Having one person spend a day desperately trying to catch up with a happily oblivious other will not lead to a serene atmosphere around the camp stove. Friendships can be ruined in a single week-end. Don't let it happen to yours!

I can't speak about the joys or not of touring in a larger group – a group of three is the largest I've ever cycled with – but the same prin-ciples will apply. Talk to each other about what you'd like to do, what

you'd like to see, how you'd like to get there. And hopefully you'll
come back better friends than when you started.

CHAPTER 16

Travelling With Your Bike

Eventually, you're going to want to start your trip from a point other than your front door. What follows is a brief overview of travelling with your bike on buses, trains and ferries in the UK and Europe, mainly France. The websites linked in the text are also listed in Appendix 1 for ease of reference.

The best advice I can give to readers outside the UK is to visit the excellent website of The Man In Seat 61, a comprehensive resource on travelling by ship and train all over the world.

I cannot say anything from personal experience about air travel, but the Cyclists' Touring Club site offers advice on how to prepare and pack your bike if travelling by air. Always check restrictions on the airline company's website.

The following focuses on train and ferry travel in the UK and Europe.

Trains

UK mainline train travel

Bikes can be brought on trains free of charge on UK services, but designated stowage space varies wildly. It is wise to make a reservation as far ahead as possible. Individual operators have their own regulations about travelling with bikes, and these may change. Whether you book your journey online or at a station, make sure you check the onboard facilities of the rail companies. Many companies will not carry bicycles at particular times of day, and most will not take tricycles, tandems and trailers unless stated otherwise in their guidelines. Currently, for example, East Coast carry tandems if two spaces have been reserved; Virgin can only carry tandems on certain train types. The National Rail guidance page gives general information on travelling with bicycles on trains. A to B magazine's website provides an excellent summary of the restrictions applying on all UK rail companies.

Eurostar

There is a cost to transporting your bike from St Pancras, London by Eurostar to Europe, whichever method you use.

To be certain your bike travels with you on the train, you can pre-book a cycle space for £30. You drop your bike off at the St Pancras International luggage office, receive a collection ticket, and then pick it up from the luggage collection area of the station you are travelling to, which will be either a luggage office or a signed location on the platform. This is by far the simplest option to choose if you are cycling to a train station and will be cycling onward from your arrival station.

You can send your bike as registered luggage, also for £30. This means that you can send it a day or two ahead, if that is convenient for you.

You can pack it in a bike bag – wheels, pedals, saddle and handlebars removed or turned to reduce bulk – and carry or send it as registered luggage for a fee of about £10. The bike bag must not exceed 120 cm in any direction, i.e., the longest part of your frame should be less than 120 cm.

The size restrictions and guidelines have changed several times since 2012, so make sure to check the official Eurostar guideline page for the most up-to-date information.

France: TGV and local train services

Travelling on intercity TGV normally requires your bike to be in a bike bag, for which there is no charge. Spaces are limited for assembled bicycles and must be reserved in advance.

Local services sometimes have spaces for bicycles, sometimes not. Always check when you purchase your ticket. In practice, in our experience, even when the train has been replaced by a bus, our anxious enquiries have been met with a shrug and a helpful heave of the machine onto the train or into the bus luggage compartment.

The Man In Seat 61 is a great site for rail and ship travel worldwide, with a page that links to detailed pages on travelling by train with your bike in different parts of Europe.

Ferries

Scottish ferries

Taking your bike on Scottish ferries is a wonderful experience, and opens up all the islands to your questing wheels. Almost all the major ferries serving the islands are run by Caledonian MacBrayne (CalMac). Bikes are carried free of charge with foot passengers; crew members will secure them in the car deck. We've always found staff extremely helpful.

If you are driving onto the islands with the intention of cycling on from there, you must declare on booking if your bikes are on the roof of your vehicle. They may have to be removed and stowed elsewhere for the crossing. (If you're wondering why you would take your vehicle onto an island when you intend to island-hop by bike from then on, it's because your vehicle will be as safe, if not more safe, parked up on one of the islands for a couple of weeks than in a secure car park on the mainland, depending upon where you start from. And the ferry ticket for your car might well be cheaper than the cost of secure parking.)

The CalMac Hopscotch ticket is worth considering if you plan to island hop, but do the sums to make sure you really need it. You can take a lot of ferry journeys before the combined cost of the tickets exceeds the cost of the Hopscotch.

Other Ferries

Most of our experience has been on Corsica Ferries and Brittany Ferries. On most ferries operating from the UK bikes travel free but a supplement may apply; Irish Ferries, for example, charge £9 at time of writing. In all cases you'll usually need to reserve a bike space. A To

B has a helpful page listing the restrictions applying on all ferry companies operating from the UK.

Bear in mind when planning that space may not always be available; spaces fill up quickly for passage to northern Spain and France from the UK during the weeks of the Tour de France, for example.

Some general advice on travelling with your bike on trains and ferries

Be aware that the calm air of advice on company websites might not be reflected in the demeanour of fellow passengers and guards on trains if, for instance, you have located where your reserved bicycle should be and manage to heave it on board only to find that its designated space is occupied by passengers and a mountain of luggage. In these instances we have generally had much more positive experiences in France than in the UK. When lifting loaded bikes on and off on regional trains in France, we have been indebted time and again to many kind people who assisted us and told us to be 'tranquille'.

If you need to change trains on your journey, I recommend that you double-check when booking whether or not you will be changing at a terminus. If not, a little extra research may reveal that your train terminates only a couple of stops from your original change station, in which case you might want to arrange your journey to change at the terminus instead. It won't always be possible, but it helps immensely to have time to embark and disembark in the relative calm of a terminal station. The experience of wheeling a laden bike frantically along a platform as the train approaches, trying to spot the cycle stowage area, then unloading some panniers so that you can actually heave the bike onboard, getting out to the platform to retrieve those panniers, getting back on, then unloading all the rest of your luggage and stowing it around the bicycle while other passengers with luggage are trying to move around your frazzled person, is not one I can recommend.

On long train journeys when we have dismantled our bikes, we carry all the panniers in two hockey bags which we stow in the normal luggage compartments on the trains.

When travelling on vehicular ferries between countries, you'll generally board at the vehicle entrance, where staff will (with varying degrees of politeness) indicate where you can leave your bike. In most cases they will secure it to rails on the bulkheads themselves.

Though we originally had qualms about letting our bikes out of our sight on ferry car decks, we have never found security to be an issue, as those decks are locked to passengers from 15 minutes after departure to 15 minutes before arrival. We only take our bar bags and perhaps a pannier up to the passenger decks, depending upon the duration of the ferry trip.

CHAPTER 17

Safety and Security

L ike a horse that must be secured and fed and watered before
you turn your attention to your own needs, your bike is your
steed and must be safe and secure before you can relax. If you
are actually touring, by which I mean being a tourist on a bicycle,
you'll sometimes want to leave your bike to wander around exploring
the village, town or wherever it is that you've stopped.

You should have a good lock. I've been using the same combination lock for the last 20 years. The wire loop is just about long
enough to go through both of my wheels and around a fixed object
such as a bike park, telegraph pole or railings. The standard advice
given is to use two locks of differing types to deter opportunistic
theft, as thieves will rarely carry around tools to attack both a combination wire lock and a D-lock, for example. However, locks are heavy.
I've never carried two locks but you should bear this advice in mind,
particularly if you are going to heavily populated areas, or have any
doubts about the levels of bike crime in the area you are planning to
visit. You might want to ride right into the middle of London or
Edinburgh, and if the fancy takes you, then do it! But take sensible
precautions.

When we travel together, Adi and I both use combination locks, made of strong, thick covered wire. We pass each lock through the front wheel of one bike, the back of the other and through the frame, sometimes also passing through the handles of the panniers. This means that they are relatively secure even if there is no fixed object to lock them to; it would be very obvious to passers-by if someone was attempting to steal them. We choose a well-lit and busy spot and take our bar bags away with us, which contain our most valuable items – money, credit cards, phones, cameras, passports. As we enjoy exploring, we've done this in countless places without any mishaps.

Travelling solo it's a little more difficult, and you might want to invest in a second lock; the peace of mind might be worth the extra weight. Do whatever makes you happy, but be sensible. Following a few of the precautions above will ensure that, unless you are very unlucky, your bike and your possessions should be safe. Don't let concerns about security stop you from trying out cycle touring.

If You Need Further Encouragement

I hope that if you've read this far you are already planning a cycle touring trip, maybe your first overnighter. Actually, that's untrue: I hope that at some point in the first few chapters you put this aside and actually went and did it. But if you have read this book through and are still undecided about whether or not cycle touring is for you, let me offer some further encouragement.

Your mental well being

Cycle touring brings all decisions down to the most basic: where to go and how to get there. Every time I ride out of my house with a pannier on the back, whether it's to a hostel in the mountains less than twenty miles away or for a mini-tour over a weekend, there is a peace that descends upon me as I roll down that first bit of road. All other decisions are left behind.

A fresh perspective

You will see parts of your world, however big or small that is, that you wouldn't have seen any other way.

The most amazing scenery can be seen better from the back of a bike than from inside a car, and that scenery, whether it's an unexpected castle in a small Welsh town or the spur of a tree-clad mountain, looks just as majestic when glimpsed through thick fat clouds as it does when lit in brilliant sunshine.

We were thrilled, one chilly May day in Glen More on the Isle of Mull, to see a pair of golden eagles appear during a break in the rain clouds above us. If we'd stayed in the campsite that morning as we'd been tempted to do, we'd never have seen those eagles as we crouched out of the wind just below the top of the pass, sipping from our flask of tea. These moments are what it's all about. That, and being able to eat your own body weight every night.

Cycle tourers are a friendly bunch

At a campsite when other tourers ride up it is always great to go over and see where they have been, what they have seen, and, most importantly, to see what kind of kit they are using: what kind of tent; what kind of cooking stove; sleeping bags, bikes, panniers. At some point the conversation will turn to the odd thing that you've noticed them using or doing. 'Em, do you mind me asking – what exactly is that?' And you'll have found your own unique cycle touring tip.

You'll feel the shape of the land underneath you

Discovery is just under your nose, wherever you live. And when you are confident you can plan longer escapades: around the coast of your county or your country; choosing a random river and following it from source to sea; crossing a country from east to west. Riding through the land immerses you in its shapes. That sense of newness, of the world constantly changing around you – its views, its smells, its sounds, the feel of it passing under you – is a wonderfully seductive state: thrilling and relaxing in equal measure.

And anyone can do it.

All you need is a bicycle.

Appendix 1: Resources

This section contains all of the resources mentioned in the book, as well as other websites and books that you may find useful.

BOOKS

Food and Maintenance

Amy-Jane Beer & Roy Halpin, *Moveable Feasts*, Cicerone, Milnthorpe, 2008

Mel Allwood, *The Total Bike Maintenance Book*, Carlton Books, London, 2012

Cycle Touring Tales

Ellie Bennett, *Mud, Sweat and Gears*, Summersdale Publishers, Chichester, 2012

Andrew P. Sykes, *Crossing Europe on a Bike Called Reggie*, CyclingEurope.org, 2012

Mike Carter, *One Man And His Bike*, Ebury Press, 2012

Planning Long Cycle Tours

Friedel and Andrew Grant, *The Bike Touring Survival Guide*, TravellingTwo, 2011

Celebrating the Bicycle

Bella Bathurst, *The Bicycle Book*, HarperCollins, 2011

Robert Penn, *It's All About The Bike*, Particular Books (Penguin), 2010

WEBSITES

Cycle Touring Websites

www.alastairhumphreys.com/microadventures-3:
Alastair Humphreys is an advocate of the adventures waiting to happen just under your nose.

cyclingeurope.org: The blog of Andrew Sykes and his bike Reggie.

travellingtwo.com: The hugely informative website of the authors of The Bike Touring Survival Guide

Accommodation

Hostels
Youth Hostel Association UK: www.yha.org.uk
Independent Hostel Guide UK: independenthostels.co.uk
Scottish Independent Hostels: www.hostel-scotland.co.uk
Gatliff Hebridean Hostels Trust: www.gatliff.org.uk
Hostelling International: www.hihostels.com

Camping
Scottish Outdoor Access Code and wild camping:
www.visitscotland.com/see-do/activities/walking/wild-camping

Camping, including wild camping, in and near National Parks in England and Wales: www.nationalparks.gov.uk/visiting/camping

Cool Campsites, UK and Europe: www.coolcamping.co.uk

Campsites UK: www.ukcampsite.co.uk

Public Campsites in the US and Canada: www.uscampgrounds.info

Travelling by train

General information from National Rail on travelling with bicycles on trains in the UK: www.nationalrail.co.uk

A To B's excellent summary of the restrictions applying on all UK rail companies: www.atob.org.uk/bike-rail/uk-bike-rail-restrictions

The Man In Seat 61's hub page for British trains with links to more detailed pages on transporting your bike by train in various parts of Europe: www.seat61.com/bike-by-train.htm

The official Eurostar guideline page: http://www.eurostar.com

Travelling by ferry

Restrictions applying to bicycles on a selection of UK ferry operators: www.atob.org.uk/bikeferry-2/uk-bike-ferry-restrictions

Clothing

Minx Girl: www.minx-girl.com

Georgia In Dublin: www.georgiaindublin.com

Café du Cycliste: www.cafeducycliste.com

Appendix 2: Our Check List

These are all of the items that we have brought with us over the years, though not all at the same time! What we actually select to bring from this list, particularly from the clothes list, will vary according to the duration of the trip and where we will be going.

Bike, Accessories, Tools and Repairs

- Bicycle!
- Lock
- Spare inner tube, 1 each
- Tyre levers, 2-3
- Puncture repair kit
- Emergency credit card
- Multi-tool with hex keys 2-8 mm, flat-head and cross-point screwdrivers, and a star key

For trips longer than a weekend:

- Two gear cables
- Two brake cables
- Set of brake pads for each bike
- Chain oil
- Latex disposable gloves (optional)

General purpose tools and repair kit

- Gaffer tape
- Spare nuts and bolts
- Leatherman-style or Swiss Army-knife style multi-tool
- Tie straps, various widths

- Bungee cords
- Tent pole repair kit

Tent and Camping Accessories

- Tent
- Groundsheet
- Sleeping mat
- Sleeping bag
- Sleeping bag liner
- Pillow or pillow substitute
- Lamps and torches
- Tablecloth and spacemats

Cooking

- Stove, fuel and fuel bottle
- Stove windbreaks
- Saucepan with grab handle
- Kettle
- Sharp knives and sharpening stone
- Mixing spoon and/or spatula
- Lightweight sporks (combined spoon and fork)
- Small plastic bowl
- Plastic chopping board
- Camping mugs, insulated
- Camping plates
- Coffee percolator
- Lighter
- Washing up liquid
- Sponge

- Towel
- Laundry liquid

Food

- Store cupboard: salt, pepper, spice and herb mixes, tea bags, coffee
- Emergency stash of oatcakes and/or cereal bars
- Water bottles

Clothing

- Cycling shorts
- Cycling skirt
- Breathable cycling jerseys or other breathable outdoor tops, short and long sleeved
- Warm top or fleece
- Waterproof jacket
- Waterproof leggings
- Arm and leg warmers
- Light-weight walking trousers with zip-off legs
- Off-bike top and skirt
- Sandals
- Cleated cycling shoes or sandals
- Walking boots
- Trainers
- Headband
- Neck-buff
- Gloves
- Hats — sun hat/cycling hat/woolly hat
- Overshoes

- Cycling tights
- Helmet if required in country of travel
- Reflective strap

Wash Bag

- Face moisturiser
- Eye cream (I'm at that age)
- Toothpaste and toothbrush
- Face wash
- Shower-gel
- Shampoo and conditioner
- After-sun and/or body moisturiser
- Sunscreen, waterproof
- Miniature hairbrush with tiny mirror
- Lip balm
- Deodorant

First Aid Kit

- Painkillers such as paracetomol and ibuprofen
- Assorted adhesive plasters
- Rectangular and triangular bandages (non-adhesive)
- Sterile gauze (for binding bandages)
- Hydrocortisone/antihistamine cream, for treatment of insect bites and stings
- Small pair of scissors
- Tweezers
- Waterproof sunscreen
- Insect repellent

Maps, Guides and Other Books

- E-reader
- Regional guidebooks
- Maps
- Satnav
- Novels
- Other guidebooks
- Notebooks and pens

Miscellaneous

- Mobile phone
- Front and rear lamps
- Head torch
- Bike computer
- USB charging cables for phone, camera, e-reader and other electronic devices
- Three-pin plug with USB socket
- Two-pin converter (for France and Europe)
- Spare batteries for head torch, lamps and bike computer

Acknowledgements

This book is the result of many miles pedalled and many kind people encountered. Most of the time we never exchanged names, but I saw their faces in my mind and heard their voices in remembered snatches of conversation while I was writing this book. I would like to thank them all.

I'm grateful to friends and family who encouraged me to write the book, especially my sisters Noreen and Theresa Madigan, who looked over the text and made suggestions, gently drawing my attention to idiocies and assumptions committed. Any remaining quirks or errors are entirely my own.

Finally, I want to thank Adi Moore, who encouraged me to do it, supplied chocolate and cake at sanity-saving intervals, and who always waits for me at the top of the hill.

ABOUT THE AUTHOR

Marie Madigan is an Irish writer and nature conservationist living in North Wales, who spends most of her time walking, cycling and writing. It is her ambition to cycle along every road marked in yellow on the Ordnance Survey map of the UK.

Did you enjoy this book? An honest review left wherever you bought it is always welcome, and really important for indie authors! The more reviews an indie book gets, the easier it is to promote and reach new readers. Even a line or two at the store where you bought it, or on Goodreads, would be an enormous help.

Want some more of Marie Madigan's work for free? Subscribers to her mailing list get a free digital copy of Southern France In Low Gear and a free Countdown To Your Cycle Tour Check List in PDF. You'll only be contacted when there is an offer, news or a new book is about to be released. Your email address will never be shared and you can unsubscribe at any time. Find out more:

www.mariemadigan.co.uk

Other Books

A Slow Tour Through France

When Marie and her partner Adi spent two months cycling around France with a tent, they weren't trying to break any records; they just wanted a bit of sunshine for a change.

France enchanted, but the weather had other ideas. During nearly 2,000 slow miles they struggled with hailstones, hills, bad knees, and the scarcity of tea pots - only to find, as if they didn't know it already, that no matter what the weather and the road throw at you, life is still better on the back of a bike.

Southern France In Low Gear

During a cycle tour in France in 2012, Marie's legs started talking to her. A year later, pedalling up the first long hill in Corsica, The Legs piped up again.

'And how long is it for this time? Two months? And we're going where? Oh, just to the Atlantic. Fine. No problem.'

With the same sturdy old bikes, the same stoic Legs and the same measure of stubbornness and stamina, Marie and Adi chug around Corsica, pedal through Provence, skirt the Cévennes and plod through the Pyrenees. With encounters with booted eagles, friendly farmers, cycle tourers of all description and a thrilling glimpse of the Yellow Jersey, the hilly regions of France charm them once again.

A Short Ride Round North Wales

Proving to themselves that a cycle tour needn't be a cross-continental expedition, Marie and Adi pedal out of their front gate and off into the Welsh summer. Six short days spin out into miles of lanes, criss-crossing borderland valleys and majestic uplands where they discover new lanes and vistas in their home of North Wales, rediscover old ones, and remind themselves once again that there's no better way of exploring than on the back of a bike.

Say Hello!

Visit Marie's website at mariemadigan.co.uk, where you can download a free 'Countdown To Your Cycle Tour Check List' and a free digital copy of Southern France In Low Gear.

You can follow her on Twitter: twitter.com/mariethemadigan

Or email Marie at marie@mariemadigan.co.uk

Made in the USA
San Bernardino, CA
23 August 2019